REFLECTIONS ON TRANSCENDENCE

REFLECTIONS ON TRANSCENDENCE

Everything You Have Been Searching for Is Already Inside of You

ELIZABETH M. LYKINS

Paintings by Steven D. Lyons

Transcendence Publishing

Second Edition - Reflections on Transcendence
First Printing in 2022
ISBN 9798218081904 (Paperback)
ISBN 9798218081911 (ePub)
Transcendence Publishing
www.amagnificentmetamorphosis.com

First Edition - Reflections on Transcendence
Copyright © 2020 by Elizabeth M. Lykins
First Edition printing - 2020 by Austin Macauley Publishers

For my daughter, Caroline, who has
taught me more about life than she will ever know.

Contents

Foreword

I would like to thank the late, Steve Lyons, for the generous use of his paintings in Reflections on Transcendence. Steve's kindness and compassion for others are tangible in his vast catalog of thought-provoking paintings. Those of us who knew and loved Steve, miss him very much. I am grateful for Steve's staff, collaboration, and support during the creation of the First Edition.

The Second Edition of Reflections on Transcendence, is dedicated to the memory of Steve Lyons, who left us after a valiant battle with brain cancer in March, 2021, just six months after the First Edition was published. In the Second Edition, Steve's paintings and life's work live on, to inspire others and to continue his creative legacy. This revised edition has been edited and reformatted with additional updates to more accurately reflect the intention of the first edition and to enhance the reader's experience.

A Word from Elizabeth and Steven

"Being who you really are, is very liberating. An authentic life is un-encumbered by the expectations and desires of others, without the need to conform to what anyone thinks you ought to be. When we arrive into this world, we view everything with wonder and awe, without any feelings of self-loathing or inadequacy. It does not take too long before we become conditioned by the contaminated thinking of the world around us and deceived into believing that we are flawed, incomplete beings. This belief about ourselves is a fundamental misunderstanding of our true nature.

I have enjoyed a lengthy career in the service of others as a medical provider, writer, and transformational coach, while on my own con-voluted journey of self-discovery. I have walked along different paths and traveled to distant places in an attempt to find truth and lasting happiness. Along the way, I discovered answers in the most unexpected places. As I directed my attention inward instead of looking outside of myself for answers, I began to realize that the happiness that I was seeking had been within me all along. I just could not see it. It is only within the sacred sanctuary of one's inner-self, where lasting happiness can be found."

– Elizabeth Lykins

"I think there are painters and artists. The former is committed to creating imagery with paint; an artist is simply committed to creating. I consider myself the latter because, very simply, I must create to be happy, a fact I learned and accepted at a very young age. I most often create through concept and metaphor and my goal is always the same: to translate the energy of a subject through color and textured dimensionality because creating, for me, is about feeling, not seeing, and I hope to trigger emotional responses in viewers of my work.

To that end, I create sculptural paintings, images that are highly dimensional and tactile. The technique is a reinvention of the 15th century *impasto* technique and this heightened dimensionality in my work is organic to me because it is how I experience the world; as a dimensional, tactile environment.

At the end of the day, I hope people see me as an artist, who helped push art along through my innovative techniques and who helped others recognize and honor the creative process. Being creative is good for one's soul and for the souls around you."

– Steven Lyons

Intention

The intent of this compilation of thought-provoking imagery and accompanying verse, is to facilitate a unique and deeply emotive experience in the reader. Embarking on a reflective journey within, presents an opportunity to experience a dynamic shift in one's current thinking. This body of work is not intended to be read in chronological order. Browsing the pages, as you may feel moved for inspiration is encouraged. Our hope is that you will surrender fully to what you see and feel, allow personal insights to well up from within you, and permit them to make their way into the forefront of your consciousness.

What People Are Saying

"Although the words and the art within this book are beautiful and are certainly soul-stirring, the true magnificence of Elizabeth and Steven's work and the source of innate resilience and well-being is not found there between the pages...This book sets the reader off on an exploration of epic proportions, within and without. I, wholeheartedly, recommend this book to be read; but not cover to cover. Dip in and then take some time and space to reflect... It is in these reflective moments and in the spaces between the chapters, between the words and the stunning art, that the power of this book lies... Read a bit and then sit in silence and let it soak in!" – Robin Lockhart, Therapeutic Coaching, Recipient of the 2016 Global Youth Worker of the Year award, by The Commonwealth

"The book is a beautiful compilation of ancient, timeless wisdom from many sources. I really enjoyed the concept and format of this book. The range of wisdom shared was truly impressive! I always enjoy reading how each of us uniquely presents with words what we see of the Three Principles." – Linda Sandel Pettit, Ed D, Counseling Psychologist

"Do yourself a big favor and get your hands on the remarkable new book by Elizabeth M. Lykins, Reflections on Transcendence. The vital message of the book, which Lykins explores from a number of different angles, is that life is best understood and lived from an inside-out perspective; that external circumstances are not the source of our experience; good, bad, or indifferent, and that we cannot expect to find what we seek (wellbeing, happiness, the meaning of life, or solutions to our 'problems') anywhere other than within ourselves. Expressed another way, it is the inside-out perspective that offers the best chance of living to the fullest, in the full understanding that it is our thoughts, not the past or future or the seduction of what's 'out there', which are the agents responsible for our experience and those thoughts only acquire whatever significance and relevance to our lives that we elect to assign to them, because the truth of who we are, our essence, is never to be found in the random thoughts that occur to us and frequently sabotage our ability to live in the moment and respond spontaneously to what's available in the here and now. Dramatically illustrated by Steven D. Lyons, this important new book has the potential to transform your understanding of the human experience and offers a roadmap to a more peaceful and effortless life." – Dr. John Countryman, Retired Theatre professor, Berry College. Recipient of two Kennedy Center, American College Theatre Festival Awards for Directing

"We all go through life with our thoughts swimming around in our minds and they define our lived experience. The bad ones pull us down and have undesirable ripple effects. Elizabeth, in Reflections on Transcendence helps us navigate those troubling thoughts or state of mind. It is divided into short chapters, comprising of common thoughts and emotions, which prevail in our minds from time to time, accompanied by art work relating to those.

Whenever you want to feel differently, pause whatever you are doing. Shut your eyes, take three deep breaths, and open the book at the relevant theme chapter. Just read what's in there and ask yourself, "What's the message here? What do I know differently now?" And let your mind answer in its own time. Take the book with you in your smartphone, tablet, or laptop. You never know when you may need it."
– Aamer Iqbal, MD, Asthma Specialist, and Certified Wellness Coach

"I think it is outstanding; The best 3P based access to wellbeing I have read." – Bill Cumming, Director, The Boothby Institute and The Pause Place

"As I read through the pages, I was filled with so many thoughts and emotions of the years of my life. Funny how you can read quotes or words of wisdom and be taken back to a specific moment in life. Instantly, you are back at a precise moment, where you had an experience. Reading through 'Reflections of Transcendence' was similar to taking a trip through my life's emotions log book. There were flashbacks to moments, places, people, experiences, that I had neatly, or not so neatly, tucked away, never to access again. or so I thought. I would liken the words of this book to having a personal guidance counselor; one who allows the freedom to walk through the days of life in privacy and attempt to unlock one's personal journey. This book took me on a journey through my personal suitcase." – Celia McBride, RN, Emergency Medicine Nurse

"Reflections on Transcendence is pointing in one direction, where the human experience is really coming from. It's like going on a journey, its beautiful artwork helps engage the creative mind, whilst the words gently guide you to your own insights and realizations. Be prepared to get comfortable, open your mind, and be open and curious about what you are hearing from inside. Enjoy the journey." – Clésia Mendes, Speaker and Mindset Head Coach

"Like everything Elizabeth Lykins does, this is a book written with passion and intelligence. It is a wonderful guide into understanding concepts of mindfulness and a beacon of light for those searching for answers." —Meredith Broderick, MD, Sleep Medicine Specialist/ Neurologist

I

The Three Principles

The place to start for any meaningful transformation is to gain a better understanding of the role of Thought. Thought determines how we view the world and how we create our perception of the world around us. Misunderstanding how thought works and how it can either work for us or against us, is at the root of every single problem that we have in our life.

You may have been taught that your thoughts are either 'good' or 'bad'. You have also likely been taught that good or bad thoughts determine whether or not you are a good person or a bad person, that external circumstances in your life determine your destiny, and that you have no chance to change your lot in life.

This is a very big, yet innocent misunderstanding.

What does that mean?

There are Three Principles that can explain the link between mortality, the world of form, and the formless, spiritual nature of every living thing. These principles explain how each and every one of us recognizes and creates our unique experience in life from the inside-out. We are conditioned to believe that it is our circumstances in life that dictate who we are, which creates a reactionary outside-in approach to life. The outside-in approach to life is the cause of considerable suffering and unhappiness. Gaining an understanding of the inside-out nature of life, unlocks the door to happiness and limitless potential.

So, what is a principle?

A principle is a fundamental truth, something that is always true for everyone and everything. One principle that we all are very familiar with, is the principle of gravity. Whether you believe it exists or not, the entire universe is affected by its force. Gravity does not need your approval or belief; its effects are present regardless of how you feel about it.

In the same way that gravity is a principle that affects everyone and everything, there are Three Principles that explain the relationship between the mind and the body; or in other words, the formless, spiritual self, and the mortal body. These principles, as articulated by the philosopher Sydney Banks, are the principles of Universal Mind, Universal Consciousness, and Universal Thought or commonly known as Mind, Consciousness, and Thought.

THE MIND

The Universal Mind is, sometimes referred to as Divine Intelligence, God, The Spirit, Holy Spirit, The Great Spirit, The Force, and other names depending on your culture and upbringing, all referring to the same entity. Mind or the Collective Mind is the formless, nameless, eternal intelligence, and creator of all living things in our universe. Every living thing is connected to this Force that has always been and has granted us the great gift of mortality.

At the moment of our birth into the mortal world, a formless, spiritual entity, Innate Wisdom or The Force, remains within us, connecting us directly to the Universal Mind that created us. It resides within every living thing, whether or not we choose to acknowledge or accept its existence. It is always there, working quietly within us, as we experience mortality.

The purpose of this innate wisdom is to guide us through mortal life in partnership with our Creator. No one has to earn this gift. It is already within every living thing. In spite of what you may have been taught, no religious doctrine or 'salvation' is necessary to receive or possess this magnificent innate wisdom.

This formless gift of life lives within each and every one of us, housed within our mortal form. Albert Einstein understood this principle as *matter cannot be created or destroyed: $E=mc^2$*. While matter can change form, it has always existed and cannot be destroyed. The essence of who we really are, is timeless. No one is any more privy to innate wisdom or our connection to the spiritual world than any other. Each of us comes 'hardwired' with this amazing gift.

Science has no plausible explanation for this phenomenon that cannot be easily explained with the intellect alone, yet the scientific and mathematical communities know of its existence. Quantum physics is a growing field that speaks of the nature of a greater force. This is information that we can comprehend innately, without the use of scientific theories or words. This knowledge has been described in various ways in one version or another, within every culture.

There is something within us that is far greater than our mortal body.

The good news is, the human mind has the inherent capability to remain connected to the Universal Mind, throughout every moment of our time here on earth. This gift is a constant reminder of the spiritual nature of our origin, there to guide us through any situation when we are receptive to it. At the same time, we are also given the gift of free will, to do with this gift what we choose to do, creating our own unique version of life.

It is important to comprehend that the Universal Mind is an impersonal, constant, unchanging entity, equally accessible to all beings, regardless of behavior or merit. Conversely, the personal mind or the brain changes constantly, moving from thought-to-thought, moment by moment, in every living being.

The personal mind is restless, constantly making connections and associations, seeking meaning, and striving for survival and identity. Just like an amazing computer, the brain is always 'on' with millions of random thoughts passing through it day to day, changing from moment to moment. Thoughts cannot be controlled. They come to our consciousness as associations or patterns that are recognized by the brain. They are only 'good' or 'bad', if we focus on them with our complete attention, while creating new thoughts that give them life and meaning from our own imagination. Actions determine whether thoughts are good or bad, not the thoughts themselves. Thoughts are merely data contained within the amazing computer, that is our brain.

The mind and the brain are actually distinctly different entities. The brain is necessary for survival in this mortal world, while the mind or the *essence* behind the scenes of our mortal existence is *much* more significant than the brain. The mind or our spiritual self is our link to Collective Thought and Intelligence; a far more powerful force than anything that one solitary human brain could accomplish on its own.

The brain or individual intellect is only a very small part of our mind. The brain is intended to be a servant to the mind, not the master. While this may seem ethereal and a bit mind-boggling to understand intellectually, if you pay close attention to your inner voice as you read these words, you will recognize this concept as something that you have known all along but could not easily articulate.

This deeper connection to the spiritual realm is so eloquently described in William Wordsworth's 536 Ode, Intimations of Immortality from Recollections of Early Childhood, (Arthur Quiller-Couch, ed. 1919. The Oxford Book of English Verse: 1250–1900):

Our birth is but a sleep and a forgetting
The Soul that rises with us, our life's Star,
Hath had elsewhere its setting
And cometh from afar
Not in entire forgetfulness
And not in utter nakedness
But trailing clouds of glory do we come
From God, who is our home.
Heaven lies about us in our infancy!

UNIVERSAL CONSCIOUSNESS

Universal Consciousness or Awareness, as it is called in some cultures, is the gift of knowing that we exist...that we are alive; the ability to be aware of our surroundings. We are born with five senses that can help us to interpret and make sense of our existence here. The moment that we are born, this gift allows us to realize that we exist in this world of form.

There are varying degrees of consciousness that can allow us to understand more deeply, who we really are. We arrive in this life with this awareness. As we experience mortal life, consciousness about who we really are, can become hidden to us with the passage of time. Most of us spend a great deal of our adult life looking and longing for something to give our life meaning. *The meaning of life that you may be seeking, has been within you all along.* As you gain an understanding of your true nature, you can discover what you have been seeking in the most unlikely of places; within yourself.

THOUGHT

Thought is an amazing power that is possessed by every living thing. It creates our own unique perception of the world around us. No two people ever see the world in exactly the same way, as we each have our own individualized perception of the world around us. What we understand about our life is completely thought-generated and is our own creation.

How we perceive life via our thoughts is very much like watching a movie on a big screen. We interpret the images as reality, based on our perceptions of them, as they unfold before us. In reality, the images we see are analogous to digital images or pixels on a computer. They are projected on a screen by a sophisticated projector that the eyes can discern with sounds that the ears can hear, while organized and further interpreted by the brain. Our thoughts about what we are experiencing are *indirect* interpretations of what our senses are telling us directly. The brain can help us to determine whether our experience is a representation of events, like a movie or is one that is actually occurring in real time, right in front of us.

What we do with our thoughts from moment to moment, can either act as a bridge and constant connection between spiritual and mortal life or they can become a selfish master, with a life of their own. Thoughts can maintain a connection with our inner spirit or easily separate us from who we really are.

How we manage our thoughts from moment to moment, determines the type of life that we experience here on earth. Lending our attention to positive thoughts creates an entirely different life experience than one that focuses on negative thoughts. Over-analyzing, ruminating, and dwelling on negativity in the past, present, or future, creates a hell of our own making that is entirely generated by our own thoughts.

So, what does all of this mean and why should you care?

From the time of our arrival here, our thoughts gradually become more and more contaminated, becoming infiltrated by what is going on around us and how our brain interprets these events. The numerous processes of the brain are constantly generating random thoughts, distracting us, and preventing us from having access to the Mind; our internal compass.

These constant thoughts shape and form the life that we are creating moment by moment. The ability to maintain access with the Mind is the key to recognizing our inner spirit. Our inner spirit is infinitely more powerful in guiding us through life than the feeble powers of our mortal brain and personal intellect alone.

The good news is gaining access to the Mind is literally as close as a single thought away.

It is within the context of stillness and quieting the personal mind that one can begin to realize that all of the unhappiness, loneliness, and isolation that you may be feeling right now, have arisen innocently from a great misunderstanding about who you are and how life really works.

These Three Principles are as certain as gravity. You will not be able to comprehend their formless nature with your human intellect alone. These principles can only be understood by accessing your inner spirit in the context of silence, stillness, and reflection. As you ponder these ideas, listen intently to the promptings arising within you, bridging the gap between the mind and the brain, the mortal and the immortal, as you discover for yourself who you truly are.

"You find peace not by rearranging the circumstances of your life, but by realizing who you are at the deepest level."
- Eckhart Tolle

We can spend our entire lifetime rearranging and longing for our external circumstances to change, thinking that will improve our lives. Our life cannot change by changing our circumstances alone. It is by taking a courageous journey inward to our very core that will allow us to experience the lasting inner peace that we are so desperately seeking. Peace can only ever come from within us.

"If your eyes are opened, you will see the things worth seeing."
- Rumi

As we search for meaning in our lives, we are often deceived as to where to look for it. The next shiny object and the most popular self-help guru often captures our attention, then off we go to follow the path of yet another, all the while leaving us feeling empty.

If we open our eyes to the wonders of life around us, we will perceive the world with more clarity. This clearer understanding of life will not direct us toward others for answers. It will inspire us to direct our thoughts inward, where we will discover all of the answers we seek.

"Wisdom is knowing the right path to take...integrity is taking it."
- M.H. McKee

Each of us must reflect in solitude, if we hope to connect with our innate wisdom. Our innate wisdom will speak to us in a whisper, without words, while gently directing us toward the best path to take in any given moment. Listen closely and you can always know *exactly* what to do.

"Tenderness and kindness are not signs of weakness and despair, but manifestations of strength and resolutions."
- Kahlil Gibran

Kindness and a gentle spirit are qualities that are inherent within each and every one of us. Strive to expand your capacity to be gentle and kind, while resisting snuffing out the innate essence of who you really are. It is when we are kind, loving, and tender toward our fellow beings that we are most in alignment with our true nature.

"The way we choose to see the world creates the world we see."
- Barry Kaufman

If the glasses we use to view the world are scratched and chipped, our perceptions of the world will be very distorted. If we use pristine, crystal clear glasses to view the world, we will be able to appreciate the many wonders that life has to offer with clarity of vision. Change your view and you will change your world.

2

The Problem With Living in the Future

Anxiety can be a very crippling emotion. In the very complex world, in which we are living, there are plenty of chaotic and disturbing events that can get us caught up into a whirlwind of toxic thoughts. When thoughts of frightening possible future scenarios capture our attention, we physically experience a surge of fight or flight hormones that can take a significant toll on us, especially if these thoughts are sustained. Ongoing toxic thoughts keep the physical response fueled with the production of even more harmful hormones. When this occurs, we become engulfed in a state of anxiety, both, mentally and physically.

None of us knows what the future will hold. We can make plans about what we would like to do in our lives and set some goals that are indeed helpful at giving us some forward direction. What we often do not realize, is that these plans and goals are always subject to change as life unfolds. For example, we may have what seems to be a great goal to go to law school. The more we work toward that goal, we may receive a sudden insight that law is not really the profession we would like to pursue after all. While we made our plan with the best information available for our understanding at the time, as we learned and matured more, we came to understand more. Now, we may have come to the realization that a Master's in Business Administration and working in the international business sector is *really* what we would like to do instead.

For some of us, once a decision is made, we may become so caught up in that fixed goal that we block out any insights that are trying to steer us into another direction altogether. When we reject our insights, life can take an unanticipated turn that can create needless suffering.

Goals are meant to be guideposts, not mandates.

How we can become trapped in a fixed state of anxiety is by attempting to control the future, instead of allowing it to evolve on its own, either with or without our permission. If life does not work out exactly as we imagined, we can become agitated or angry that our goals did not materialize in the way we had meticulously planned; railing against the cosmos for letting us down. What we may fail to realize is that by resisting what already IS, we are missing out on the present moment and what it is desperately trying to teach us.

The present moment is all we ever have.

Think about that for a moment. The past is already gone. No matter how we might like to change it or resurrect it, we cannot ever repeat that exact moment. Mourning over past events and wanting to change them, creates great sadness and for some, significant depression.

Conversely, when we adopt the belief that we can only be happy when future events occur exactly as we have planned, we can become stuck in a state of anticipatory anxiety. Living in the past or in the future, results in suffering and loss of who and what is in front of us right now; the place where life is actually occurring.

What can we do about anxious thoughts?

When you recognize feelings of anxiety or irritability, stop for a moment and ask yourself what you are feeling. Realizing that nothing outside of you has any power to 'make' you feel any particular way, will allow you to see that your feelings are merely an expression of your *thoughts* at the moment or better stated, are your perceptions of circumstances, at the time. Realizing this can center you once again, allowing you to come back to this moment, where the horrors that you are imagining have not actually occurred and likely will never occur.

We are built for survival and are able to thrive in any given moment. As you remain present in *this* moment, insights arise in real time. We are all born with this amazing ability, but often unwittingly sabotage it by allowing toxic thoughts to take us over. It is wisdom at work when we realize that we can *never* control external circumstances.

We can only control how we perceive circumstances by stepping back to look at the bigger picture and by gaining an understanding that our anxiety is entirely thought-generated. Acknowledging this is usually all that is required for toxic thoughts to momentarily pass, along with the horrible feeling of dread that often accompanies them.

"We are moving into a new world and the old negativity will be left behind. Through the law of cause and effect, we can change the world, one person at a time."
- Dolores Cannon

While we may become overwhelmed with what is going on in the world around us, if we strive to remain in *this* moment, we will receive all the insight we need to dramatically change our world, moment by moment. Never underestimate the power of personal insight.

"The cave you fear to enter holds the treasure you seek."
- Joseph Campbell

There are many circumstances surrounding us, that can easily become overwhelming, if we allow ourselves to be overcome by fear. Fear is the act of ruminating over the future; a future that has not and may not ever occur exactly the way that we envision it. If we listen very carefully to what our inner spirit is telling us, we will know exactly what to do in *any* moment.

That can mean fleeing to save ourselves, waiting for a better moment to take the right action, or moving past those feelings of anxiety and fear, to allow our innate wisdom to guide us toward the discovery of a brand new world that is filled with endless opportunities.

"If you correct your mind, the rest of your life will fall into place."
- Lao Tzu

We have thousands of random thoughts that busily pass through our mind every day, that we cannot control. The mind is like a complicated computer; analyzing a vast amount of accumulated data. If we ruminate over past or future scenarios that we may feel are somehow, controlling us, we can become stuck in a negative feedback loop that in turn, creates a negative life. Allowing negative thoughts to pass through us relatively unnoticed, allows new and more beneficial thoughts to arise from within us, to take their place.

"One must be compassionate to one's self before external compassion."
- Dalai Lama

It is important to remember that we cannot express true compassion, love, or caring for others, without *first* being compassionate, loving, and caring to ourselves. These virtues can only arise from within us and emanate outward to others. They cannot be magically given to us by anyone or from any external circumstance. Feelings originate within us, not from anything outside of us.

"You cannot save people from themselves.
All you can do is stand firmly in your hopes for them, with compassion."
- Bryant McGill

It can be very challenging to watch people that we love doing things to harm themselves. We may see very clearly, the peril that they may be facing at their own hand, and be overcome with the desire to save them. We simply do not have the power to save people from themselves. We can love them, have compassion for them, and stand firmly, in our own convictions, but the ultimate choice for how they live their life is their choice alone.

This is the greatest gift... the freedom to choose our own path. As we demonstrate consistent loving compassion toward others, we may be able to impact their lives in ways that we may never know; ways that might make a difference.

3

Calm In the Storm

Circumstances in life can bare-down upon us upon us like massive waves crashing onto a rocky shoreline, slowly eroding who we are. We may feel tossed about and weather worn, finding it hard to stand our ground in the midst of constant, overwhelming chaos. It can seem that random external circumstances have power over our lives and that we are doomed to a fate determined by the whims of nature, the actions of others, or that our happiness depends on which way the wind blows. We hope for a better life, entrenched in the *"If only I had...then I would be happy"* way of thinking, which is like an endless roller coaster ride. This way of thinking leaves us with an unhealthy view of ourselves as constant victims of external circumstances.

Nothing could be further from the truth!

Like the deep currents in the ocean depths below the water's surface that are, both forceful and predictable in their direction, no matter what storms might be raging on the surface, each of us possesses an innate force that cannot be destroyed by what is going on around us. While the surface of the ocean can be chaotic, dangerous, and unpredictable, due to the violent forces of weather and natural events that constantly change the state of the surface waters, underneath the surface lies a predictable pattern of currents that governs the seas. Life forms below the surface are abundant and unharmed by the storms above, unless they venture too close to the surface or the turbulent shore-line.

A unique portion of the collective wisdom of the ages resides within us, where we can always find peaceful calm, with all of the direction we need to weather any storm that may be raging around us. While we cannot control circumstances and at times, are required to maneuver through significantly stormy situations, realize deeply that no storm lasts forever. If we remain connected to the calm inner spirit that each of us possesses, we can begin to comprehend that no power outside of us has the ability to harm us at our deepest spiritual level.

Calm thoughts give rise to wise actions. Within that state of calm, we can gain insight, moment by moment, as to what is the best decision for us right now, in the next moment, and the moment after that, without reacting to the chaos outside of us. This certain knowledge is the anchor that we can cling to, during any turbulent storm. All the direction we need is already flowing within us, just under the surface, much like the predictable deep ocean currents that direct the seas. When we are very still and intently listening, we can *know* with absolute certainty that a peaceful calm is there, ever ready to carry us to safety.

In the center of any storm, lies a haven of calm.

"You have power over your mind, not outside events. Realize this and you will find strength."
- Marcus Aurelius

We do not have any power over external events. Conversely, events have no power to cause us to think or feel any particular way, even though they may adversely affect our physical surroundings. What we *do* have is an amazing power; the power to choose the way we look at events, which, in turn, effects our feelings about them. Choose wisely, the thoughts you entertain.

"Our task must be to free ourselves by widening our circle of compassion to embrace all living creatures and the whole of nature and its beauty."
-Albert Einstein

When we minimize the importance of life in all of its forms and merely see the world as a means to meet our self-serving wants and desires, we have lost connection with our very nature. Our task in life is to love and to be loved, which includes a deep respect and compassion for all living things, of which, we are all a part.

"Integrity simply means a willingness not to violate one's identity."
- Erich Fromm

We arrive into this world, without filters or judgments about how things need to be. We begin our lives with our words and actions in congruence with who we are. Somewhere along the way, our thoughts can begin to take us off track. Integrity is conducting one's life by following the innate moral compass within each of us, while allowing this tremendous force to guide our actions in every relationship that we have; particularly, the one we have with ourselves. Perhaps, nothing is more important than that.

"It's better to walk alone, than with a crowd going in the wrong direction."
- Diane Grant

It is the greatest day of our lifetime, when we come to the realization that it is better to walk alone, than to follow the masses headed in a harmful, dark direction. To do this, takes tremendous courage and conviction. It is absolutely essential for us to remain true to our inner-self, if we wish to be happy. We are children of light and can only realize happiness, when we are following the light that is burning within us, not overwhelmed by the darkness that surrounds us.

"Resentment is like taking poison and waiting for the other person to die."
- Malachy McCourt

Harboring resentments and holding tightly onto perceived wrongs against us by others, is a cancer that slowly erodes our integrity, effecting how we view every aspect of our lives. The person, who has wronged us, is often completely unaffected by our resentment. Holding tightly onto the past can never change its course. It is only by letting go of lingering resentments from the past that one can be truly free to enjoy the present, which is the only moment that we ever really have.

4

You Are Not Alone

There may be times when we feel as though we are completely alone and thoroughly misunderstood. This feeling can feel even more magnified as close friends betray us, we lose our jobs, partners abandon us, our children grow up and venture out into the world, or our parents pass away. It may even seem that all of our feelings of sadness, isolation, and grief are caused by these events, leaving us feeling hopeless and thinking that if only those events had not occurred, then we would be happy.

Even though it may seem that circumstances are the cause of our feelings, it is important to realize that this belief is a misunderstanding. External events have no special powers to cause feelings in anyone. No matter how wonderful, or alternately, how heinous external events may be, they simply cannot *cause* specific feelings in anyone. Feelings arise from thoughts, while thoughts arise from the 'glasses' we use to view the world.

Our perception of life is an inside job.

Two people can experience the same circumstances and yet, see the situation very differently, because they are viewing the world through different lenses. Each of us has our own unique and individual perceptions. At times, our thoughts and subsequent feelings are aligned with actual circumstances. For example, if a loved one dies, it is appropriate to have feelings of loss, as we struggle to comprehend how life might be without them. The feeling of loss usually softens with time, as we accept what has happened, begin to understand how finite human life really is, and that each of us is subject to the laws of nature without exception. This thought-process is congruent with the circumstances.

Sometimes, thoughts and feelings are not aligned with circumstances. If a car suddenly pulls out in front of you while you are driving, you may become startled and have thoughts of imminent danger. Your heart races as you sense this danger and you begin to experience fear. *You instinctively slam on the brakes and successfully avert a crisis.* The fact is, we are designed to do what we need to do to survive, without even consciously thinking about it. We have an innate ability to instinctively react to save ourselves, in times of crisis. The problem is, our thoughts about this unsettling event can either develop into gratitude that we are safe and able to avoid harm or they can turn into anxiety or rage about nearly being killed, depending on how we assess the situation with the lenses we use to view the world. Our response is entirely based upon our *perception* about what happened, not the event itself.

The event itself did not have any power to cause specific feelings.

As each of us gains a deeper understanding about how our thoughts create feelings and how we are only ever feeling our *thoughts* about events occurring in any given moment, we are better equipped to allow negative thoughts to pass through us, without allowing them to take root within us. By pausing a moment to reflect as negative thoughts arise, before we act on them, we can more easily fall out of the toxic thought process that may be dominating our personal mind, to deepen the connection we have with our inner spirit. This deeper connection with self, leads to insights that transcend our intellectual capabilities.

Each of us possesses a unique portion of the vast Universal Intelligence within us.

As the brilliant scientist, Albert Einstein discovered: "Matter can neither be created or destroyed" or E=mc².

What this means in this context is while our form may change, the energy or spark of life that each of us inherently possesses, is part of a universal whole that can never be destroyed. Whether or not we understand, it does not alter the fact that this is a principle that governs all of us, similar to the principle of gravity. While we may not understand gravity, as a young toddler, each of us remembers being subject to its effects as we fell down numerous times while mastering the art of walking erect. Principles govern us without our permission. It is when we fight against these principles that life becomes challenging.

None of us are ever truly alone, even though it may seem that we are, as we pass through our darkest moments. We are all connected to one another; each of us an irreplaceable part of a greater whole. It is when we convince ourselves that we are alone in this world, that feelings of sadness, isolation, and separation can overwhelm us. While we all experience disappointment, loss, and grief during our lifetime, if we remain open to the promptings of our inner spirit, we will find all the resilience and clarity that we need to press on, under any circumstances. As we accept the importance of who we really are, we also experience a profound connection to the world that we share with billions of other fellow beings. We may even muster up the courage to reach out to others, who are in similar need of kindness and understanding.

You are never alone.

"To move the world, we must first move ourselves."
- Socrates

Any action that we take, is first preceded by a thought. Thoughts have feelings attached that can move us into action or inaction. While we cannot control how or when thoughts pop up in our human mind, we do have control over the attention we lend to them. By guarding the quality of our thoughts and the attention we give to them, we can be moved to accomplish great things. By ignoring negative thoughts that lead to negative feelings, we permit new, more positive thoughts to arise from within us to replace them. Beginning with ourselves, we can change the world, one thought at a time.

"When we look at modern man, we have to face the fact...that modern man suffers from a kind of poverty of the spirit, which stands in glaring contrast to his scientific and technological abundance; we've learned to fly the air like birds, we've learned to swim the seas like fish, and yet, we haven't learned to walk the Earth as brothers and sisters."
                    -Martin Luther King, Jr

In spite of our technological advances and knowledge, mankind is walking around in a state of disassociation from their spiritual self. The spiritual self is who we really are, while our body and human mind are merely a physical means of expressing our spiritual self. We are spiritual beings clothed in an earthly form. The challenge of mortality lies is in allowing our spirit to lead us and not permitting ourselves to be dominated by our human mind or physical body. All the knowledge in the world is lost, if we do not understand this and act accordingly. We are brothers and sisters.

"The secret of genius is to carry the spirit of the child into old age, which means never losing your enthusiasm."
                    -Aldous Huxley

Our happiness is very much affected by the ability to remain connected with who we are, before our thoughts became contaminated by misunderstanding. Recapturing and maintaining the awe, curiosity, enthusiasm, and wonder of childhood, can assist us in ridding ourselves of harmful thoughts and feelings, allowing us to experience the world in a more positive light.

"We are the cosmos made conscious."
-Brian Cox

If we could only realize for a moment who we really are, we would feel at peace within and be able to look more kindly, upon our fellow beings. While we may look upon the wonders of the universe in awe, we often do not appreciate that we are *literally* the universe in human form, each possessing a timeless, ageless, and powerful force within us.

5

⦿⧉⦾

Accept Then Act

Acceptance of one's present situation can lead to insight and direction.

It is when we accept the present moment for what it is and not
how we would like for it to be, that we can *act* as the moment dictates,
without reacting. Much of our anxiety in life comes from wishing that
the present was different, than it already is. Situations are what they
are and no amount of wishful thinking, can alter the present moment
for what it already is.

Where we *can* direct our energy, is in striving to accept the current
moment and whatever situation already exists, as if we had chosen it.
This objectivity keeps our mind at ease and allows our innate, internal
guidance system to surface, calmly letting us know how we can work
through the situation to our benefit. Reacting to circumstances is
turbulent, creating unhappiness and anger with attendant anxiety. In
contrast, if we quietly and objectively assess any given situation, we
will be better equipped to rationally choose the best action available,
at that moment; then the next and the next after that. Visceral reaction
is paralyzing, while decisive action is liberating. It is not our actions
alone that matter in the final analysis. It is the motivation and thoughts

that are driving those actions that can either transform us and shape our well-being or can defeat us.

It is important to understand that acceptance of what *is* does not mean resignation. Accepting a moment for what it is, does not mean that we are complicit with it or that we cannot do something about it. We do not have to resign ourselves to feeling victimized by horrible events or experiences in our lives. If we accept the situation for what it already is, no matter how horrible, we will have all the resilience and power we need within us to navigate whatever may come. If we are not overwhelmed by fighting a battle to change what already is; a battle that we cannot possibly win, we can, instead, use that energy to constructively work through whatever challenges exist, while keeping our inner-self intact and protected from harm. We are victors, not victims when we choose to accept, then, act wisely in any of life's events.

Each of us is far greater than any circumstances in life that may come and go. There is tremendous power in remaining in the present moment and working within it, instead of against it. The present moment is all we ever really have and where the magic of our lives begins and ends.

The present is our life.

"Silence fertilizes the deep place, where personality grows. A life with a peaceful center can weather all storms."
- Norman Vincent Peale

The power of silence is an amazing thing. It is within silence, reflection, and the absence of distraction that we are able to make contact with our spiritual center. Each of us possesses a uniquely powerful portion of the vast universe within us. Like a compass, it can navigate us through any storm. Find a few moments each day to quietly reflect and connect with your deeper self.

"Be the beacon of light in someone's darkness."
-Randi G. Fine

At times, it can seem that we are completely surrounded by the darkness of division, distrust, chaos, and the hurtful acts of others. We have a light within us that can drive away darkness and become a beacon in the night for those who have lost their way.

"In the long run, the sharpest weapon of all is a kind and gentle spirit."
-Anne Frank

Kindness and gentleness of spirit is our natural state. We have to learn how to hate and abuse others. It is through kindness and gentleness that we are able to experience our humanity. Being kind to those who are lashing out may be difficult, but kindness is the only language that can possibly bring a person to a greater understanding of who they really are and end the cycle of violence.

"All the powers in the universe are already ours. It is we, who have put our hands before our eyes and cry that it is dark."
-Swami Vivekananda

Awakening implies, suddenly, becoming aware of our surroundings and receiving insights. We spend much of our life looking outside of ourselves for direction and searching for answers, where they simply cannot be found. The collective wisdom of the ages is already within us, waiting for us to awaken to its promptings. We are only one thought away from gaining an understanding of who we really are.

"Time is like a river. You cannot touch the same water twice because the flow that has passed will never pass again."
-Tanu B. Singh

We cannot re-live the same moments or foretell exactly what the future will hold. We only have this moment that we are in right now. By realizing this profound truth, we can stop anguishing over past moments or feeling anxious about what may lie ahead. We are designed to be resilient in the context of reality. When we keep our focus on what we need to do in *this* moment, we experience insights that will propel us forward. This cannot happen when our attention is elsewhere.

6

◈

Have the Courage to Be Yourself

We arrive into this world free of expectations or overwhelming disappointments. We live entirely in the present, filled with awe and wonder at everything, when we are very young children. We laugh, we cry, we fall down, we get up, and we keep exploring. We are genuine in our interactions and express our feelings freely, at the moment that our thoughts arise. We are authentic and truthful.

Somewhere, along the line during those early formative years, we gradually begin to doubt ourselves. Our inner-self becomes ignored, as a result of accepting contaminated thoughts about who we are. Memories of words that we may have heard from people that we love and trust, begin to color who we think we are...

"You can't do that."
"You are dumb."
"You are ugly."
"You are pathetic."
"You don't belong here."
"You are never going to amount to anything"

"You are..."

It is in that awful moment that we begin to sacrifice who we are, seeing ourselves through the lens of how others judge us, not by who we truly are. We begin to mold our lives to the expectations and opinions of others; seeking their approval. We see the world from an outside-in perspective, losing our innate, inside-out perspective on life. At that point, our compass is lost.

Depression can develop, as we fixate upon undoing past events by thinking: *"If only... then things would be different."* Anxiety can overwhelm us, as we allow our thoughts to dwell on future scenarios that have not occurred and may never happen: *"I'll be happy when ..."* We plan and plan but are disappointed over and over again, as we remain trapped in this cycle. The present becomes obscured by past regrets and future longings. We have lost our grounding.

What can we do to find ourselves again?

Who we really are, is that innocent child within us that, once, was filled with wonder, imagination, creativity, playfulness, eagerness to learn new things, and genuine happiness, before the contamination of our thought processes began. There may be moments, when we briefly remember viewing life through a child's eyes. Our inner spirit is there, waiting for us to awaken to hear its joyous laughter once more. As we begin to appreciate that life can only work for our benefit when viewed from an inside-out perspective, we can become more receptive to a deeper communication with our inner self.

It takes tremendous courage to live in alignment with your authentic self; to march to the beat of your own unique drum. Being the person that others want you to be, will never bring you lasting happiness. Through private reflection, free of distraction and noise, you can find what you have been longing for your entire life...your true self. Coming face to face with your authentic self once more, will be the most defining moment of your life.

"Drink from the well of yourself and begin again."
-Charles Bukowski

Most of us search endlessly, outside of ourselves to find solace, comfort, and direction, only to have it elude us. While we may find helpful information and moments of brief comfort from others, it is only from within the depths of ourselves that answers, lasting comfort, and happiness can ever be found. There is a well of knowledge and direction inside each of us. Drink often from the well within, to find the peace and direction you seek.

"Create the highest, grandest vision possible for your life, because you become what you believe."
-Oprah Winfrey

Thoughts lead to action. How we spend our time in thought determines our behavior and what we attract in our lives. When we entertain thoughts of kindness, integrity, acceptance, non-judgment, and love of self, we are able to maintain contact with who we really are. This internal grounding allows our innate wisdom to propel us to greatness, one moment at a time.

"Until one has loved an animal, a part of one's soul remains unawakened."
-Anatole France

To have compassion and love for a being unlike ourselves, awakens us to the presence and loving capacity of our inner-spirit; something that is far nobler than our humanity alone. As we touch upon this capacity to love other beings and accept the trust that has been placed in us, we are far more likely to transcend cynicism and accept our higher nature. With this higher level of understanding, we can realize that, in spite of our varied exteriors, we are all a part of the same universal fabric of life with a desire to love and be loved. We are one earthly family, seeking connection with one another.

"When you make genuine contact with your inner spirit, there is an inner joy, an inner peace, that takes over."
-Michael Bernard Beckwith

That, which defines us as a living being, is our mysterious inner spirit. We arrive cloaked in a physical form that is foreign to us. We spend our lifetime adjusting to the physical world, while our spiritual self observes our mortal life unfolding. When we are very still and reflective, we are able to appreciate the essence of who we really are. It is in that moment of awakening that we can experience inexplicable happiness and joy that arises from within.

"Awakening is not changing who you are, but discarding who you are not."
-Deepak Chopra

When a person 'awakens' to who they really are, they begin to shift their pattern of thinking and see, clearly, what thoughts and behaviors are preventing them from being their authentic-self. Thoughts that run counter to the inner-self, distance us from our innate moral compass. Listen carefully to your inner voice. It is a reliable compass that can direct you through any crisis.

7

Still I'll Rise

What may be happening, at this very moment, in our relationships, our families, our cities, our states, or our countries, can envelope us with a dark, paralyzing uncertainty. The world is an ever-changing place with some challenges being more difficult to weather than others. Some of us may be living in fear of our lives, our jobs, our health, our safety, or completely overwhelmed by thoughts of being imminently forced out of our homes or separated from our families.

How can we keep ourselves from sinking into despair?

What is crucial to realize is that no matter what is going on around us or outside of us, *events* have no power over who we really are, internally. What that means is, that absolutely no one and no earthly power has the ability to destroy your inner spirit, without your permission. While it is true that individuals may insult you, harm you physically or emotionally, harass, threaten, or be menacing, your human spirit possesses all the clarity and wisdom you need to overcome any of these assaults.

That, which makes you who you are; the human spirit, is timeless and ageless. You already possess all of the inner fortitude and strength that you need to overcome any obstacle, at the very moment, that the need arises. Your amazing spirit can withstand any trial in life, providing you with all the necessary wisdom you need. Listen carefully to that still, small voice within you, gently attempting to gain your attention, so it can guide you. As you feel it welling up from within, you will have the courage you need, to rise up and accomplish great things that you never thought were possible.

Just like moons and like suns, with the certainty of tides, just like hopes springing high...still I'll rise.
-Maya Angelou

"The inspiration you seek is already within you. Be silent and listen."
-Rumi

We are designed to function optimally within the bounds of reality. When our thinking is not based in reality, we experience frustration, anxiety, and attract unhappy experiences. The inspiration we need to navigate life, is inherent within us. As you listen very carefully, you can hear your inner voice speaking, giving you direction in what you need to do at any given moment. All you need to do is to be silent... and listen.

"It is the mark of an educated mind to be able to entertain a thought without accepting it."
-Aristotle

It is all too easy to sink into despair, as we hear about distressing events or witness horrific images of tragedies that surround us. We have the ability to objectively view our thoughts, without accepting them. Allow them to pass through you, observing them coming and going, like a gentle breeze. Observation, without judgment, allows us to assess any situation and wisely choose appropriate action, without reacting to events.

"One person can make a difference and everyone should try."
-John F. Kennedy

It is easy to be deceived into thinking that our voice does not matter and that no one is listening to us. One solitary voice has the ability to inspire countless others into action. You have a unique voice that no one else possesses. One never knows the tremendous impact they may have on another.

"A person often meets his destiny on the road he took to avoid it."
-Jean de La Fontaine

What we avoid and criticize the most in others, are usually qualities that we recognize in ourselves; qualities that we do not want to accept. By facing our fears and anxieties head on, we have the opportunity to understand and accept them as they really are. Facing one's self is the greatest and most important challenge of our lifetime. It is also the necessary catalyst for lasting transformation.

"Feelings are much like waves, we can't stop them from coming, but we can choose which one to surf."
-Jonatan Martensson

Thoughts always give rise to feelings. They can arise fast and furious, without warning. While we cannot control which thoughts may arise, we do have a choice about which ones to surf and which ones to merely observe. Riding the high-quality thoughts and feelings, while observing the turbulent ones from a distance, will guide us safely back to solid ground.

"Courage doesn't always roar. Sometimes courage is the quiet voice, at the end of the day, saying, 'I will try again tomorrow.'"
-Mary Anne Radmacher

We often think of courage as grand acts that saves millions of lives. There are infinite possibilities to demonstrate courage, even in small ways. Courage is being afraid of taking action and doing it anyway. Courage is standing up for others, who are being harmed and not joining in, when the vulnerable are being maligned. Courage is also dusting yourself off, after you fall, and getting up just one more time. Have the courage to stand up and make a conscious choice to do the right thing.

8

Happiness Is Not Dependent On Circumstances

We come into this world free from contaminated thoughts without a darkened view of the world. We have to be taught by others to be unhappy, pessimistic, fearful, and filled with hatred. Silently observe a young child playing. In spite of their surroundings, young children are resilient, living completely in the present, without a single care for either the past or the future. As time passes, little by little, our thoughts can take us further and further away from who we really are; resourceful, happy, calm, and innately possessing the ability to know what to do, at any given moment.

By the time we reach adulthood, most of us begin to believe that circumstances control our emotions...

> *"He makes me happy..."*
> *"She makes me so angry..."*
> *"He completes me..."*
> *"If I only had a million dollars, I could..."*

What we fail to understand is, that circumstances do not have any real power to control our inner-self, unless we surrender our will to them. We simply cannot control circumstances, no more than we can control a violent storm. In spite of this lack of external control, we already possess all of the power we need to remain calm, as any storm that may be swirling around us, passes. Understanding this concept is very empowering.

Life works from the inside-out, not the outside-in.

Whenever you feel as though circumstances are taking over your life, well-being, and clarity of thought, take a moment to reflect on who you really are.

In that moment of pause, realize that any anxiety you may be feeling over circumstances, outside of your control, is only thought-generated. No storm lasts forever. The storm you may be experiencing right now, will also pass. As you remain centered, your innate resilience will assist you to maintain the happiness, calm, and peace that already resides within you, while the storm rages on around you. Happiness is our natural state. Look deeply within to find the happiness that is silently waiting for you to recognize it.

"It's the little things that are vital. Little things make big things happen."
-John Wooden

It is easy to become overwhelmed when glimpsing into what may appear to be a troubled future. If we remain in this present moment, we are more poised to receive the inner strength and wisdom that we need to make the right choices as life unfolds. It is the little things that we do, moment by moment, that matter; changing our world, one moment at a time.

"Your vision will become clear only when you look into your heart. Who looks outside, dreams. Who looks inside, awakens."
-Carl Jung

How we perceive the world depends on the lenses we use to view it. Our perception of life can be very distorted, depending on the quality of our thoughts. If we look to the world outside of us to forge our thoughts, we will be very unhappy, looking in vain for happiness. By looking within, for the answers that we are seeking, we can awaken to who we truly are, with all of the innate guidance we need to maneuver any of life's circumstances.

"Great spirits have always encountered violent opposition from mediocre minds."
-Albert Einstein

One must never fear opposition. Greatness does not come to us by seeking accolades from those around us. There will always be negative reactions from those who view life with the myopic lens of misunderstanding. Opportunities for greatness, usually, require courage and determination.

"Kindness is more than deeds. It is an attitude, an expression, a look, a touch. It is anything that lifts another person."
-Plato

Acts of kindness are more impactful than any other interaction we have with others. Actions are always preceded by thoughts. Allowing thoughts of kindness and compassion to germinate and grow within us, enables kind deeds to flow naturally. True kindness is anything that one can do to help another to be freed from the chains of their circumstances. Both, the giver and the receiver are touched in immeasurable ways, as we maintain a regular practice of expressing kindness toward others.

9

Living In the Present Moment

Most of us live our lives seeking to be anywhere other than where we are at this very moment. We may reminisce about the past longing to repair what can never be undone. Conversely, we may direct our thoughts toward a world of fantasy about an uncertain future, even setting our sights on the notion of "I will be happy when..."

In doing this, we miss out on the only place where life really occurs; this *present moment*. It is within the present moment that we discover the true magic of living, loving, and the amazing gift of life. Every being possesses an innate guidance system that allows us to navigate life with adaptability and direction about the best choice for us, at any given moment. When we direct our thoughts toward the illusory past or future, we can easily get off course and miss out on the lessons that life is trying to teach us, right now, in *this* moment, that will never be repeated.

While it is comforting to recall fond memories and to consider future possibilities, becoming locked in a past or future oriented thought pattern can keep sad memories alive or create anxiety about a variety of possible future scenarios. When this pattern of thinking comes to your awareness, recognize it for what it is. Thoughts have no power over you, unless you allow them to be expressed through actions. Pause for just a moment to become centered, observing your thoughts. By taking no immediate action, new thoughts will arise to take their place, allowing you the necessary space to enjoy this moment right now; the only moment where your life is actually happening.

"Life isn't a matter of milestones, but of moments." -Rose Kennedy

"Let no man pull you low enough to hate him."
-Martin Luther King, Jr

While hate exists in the world, our natural state is one of love. We have to be taught to hate and fear. Love is the remedy that counteracts all hateful actions. Hate is never remedied by responding with more hatred. In spite of how difficult it may be to love the unlovable, it is only love that can conquer hate.

"You will face many defeats in your life. But never let yourself be defeated."
-Maya Angelou

Perhaps, one of the more challenging aspects of life is weathering the disappointment of defeat. All of us are subject to the ebb and flow of challenges and set-backs, no matter who we are. Quietly reflect on any challenges that you may be facing right now. As you do, your innate resilience will rise up from within you, to give you all of the encouragement and guidance that you may need to overcome any challenges.

"Look within. Within is the fountain of good, and it will ever bubble up, if thou wilt ever dig."
-Marcus Aurelius

We may be feeling uneasy or restless, as we witness chaos and suffering in the world. Although we may search for happiness in the world at large, this search will leave us unsatisfied. We are looking for happiness in the wrong place. The happiness and contentment that we are seeking already exists within us, as an unending wellspring of goodness and light. All that is required for access is to look within, listen carefully to the sound of its voice, and dig, just a little bit deeper.

"A child can teach an adult three things: to be happy for no reason. To always be curious. To fight tirelessly for something."
-Paul Coelho

Young children have not yet been influenced by distorted thoughts and the misunderstanding of having an outside-in perception of life. They live entirely in the present, without any concept of past or future. Living in the moment and in sync with the inside-out nature of thought is how we arrive at true happiness and fulfillment. There is absolutely nothing outside of us that can ever give us the lasting happiness that we are seeking.

"Begin doing what you want to do now. We are not living in eternity. We have only this moment, sparkling like a star in our hand and melting like a snowflake."
-Francis Bacon, Sr

While the essence of who we are is ageless and timeless, our mortal form is not. Our time, in this form, is fleeting. No matter what your age may be, you can begin, right now, to be your genuine self and make the contributions to mankind that only you can make. Each of us is valuable to countless lives.

"We must accept finite disappointment, but never lose infinite hope."
-Martin Luther King, Jr

Disappointments in life ebb and flow, as we move through time and space. While they are a part of everyone's lives, they are always finite. That which moves us into action in the face of disappointment, is infinite hope. Hope brings us back to our innately positive state, where we have the capability to weather all things gracefully.

10

Life Is a Reflection of Your Thoughts

Most of us mistakenly believe that happiness, in life, occurs randomly, perhaps, also believing that living in abject poverty and being unhappy is something that is predetermined by the gods. This way of looking at life is an illusion.

The life that each of us creates, with our amazing personal mind, is a direct reflection of our thoughts. We paint the canvas of our mind with many colors and hues, as a result of the dominant thoughts that we entertain. The human brain is an amazing organ that can make associations and correlations, while recognizing patterns and generating endless thoughts about these patterns. However, a truly happy life is one that is governed by our inner spirit, not dominated by a volatile parade of reactions to every thought and feeling that arises within our personal mind.

Who we really are, is not limited by our human brain, alone. Each of us is an important link in the magical chain of life; with a unique contribution to make. While we have a mind, we are not our mind in the same way that we have a hand, but are not our hand. The personal mind, along with the thoughts that it generates, is merely a tool to allow us to maneuver in our mortal world. Each of us has an innate ability to either accept or reject the many thousands of thoughts that come to our consciousness each day.

By focusing on our negative thoughts, we attract even more negativity. By focusing on positive thoughts, while observing, but not accepting the negative ones, we can allow toxic thoughts to pass through us, without permitting them to take root. Like seeds blowing in the wind, thoughts can only blossom and grow, if they take root and are nurtured. If we allow life to blow seeds of negativity through us, without permitting them to land on fertile soil, we can then cultivate positive thoughts, that will blossom and grow into a beautiful garden.

When negative thoughts arise from negative situations, be aware of what is happening within you and observe them. Try not to judge them, just observe. This allows negative thoughts to pass through you, without taking hold of your mind or creating new thoughts about them. It is at that point, that your thoughts are free to formulate objective actions, instead of impulsive reactions. Harness how much attention you give to negative thoughts that arise within you, about situations surrounding you. This practice can be the pivotal change that allows you to connect more deeply with your inner-self. Everyone faces the same challenges with thoughts. Mastering how you allow random repetitive thoughts to settle within your mind, determines everything about the quality of life that you will have.

*"All that we are is the result of what we have thought. The mind is every-
thing. What we think we become."*
-Buddha

All of our actions are preceded by thought. What that means is our
behavior is based upon how we think. To live a life filled with happiness
and contentment, we must guard the quality of our thoughts. Allow
negative thoughts to pass through you, without giving them the opportunity to grow, while allowing positive ones to take root and thrive.

*"Just remember, the storm doesn't last forever. It can scare you; it can
shake you to your core. But it never lasts. The rain subsides, the thunder dies,*

and the winds calm to a soft whisper. And that moment, after the storm
clouds pass, when all is silent and still, you find peace. Quiet, gentle peace."
-S.L. Jennings

While we may face violent storms swirling around us that seem to be seeking our demise, a moment of calm always comes, as the storm subsides. This moment of calm allows you the space you need to tap into your innate spirit, where you will find answers to your problems. No storm lasts forever. Wait for the calm.

"The best and most beautiful things in the world cannot be seen or even
touched – they must be felt with the heart."
-Helen Keller

The most valuable treasure that we possess cannot be bought or sold. Our greatest treasure is the connection we share with our fellow beings. We are all connected to one another. Each of us possesses a unique portion of the Universal Spirit, whether or not we recognize it. If we listen carefully to the inner voice within, we can feel this tremendous force speaking to us in a voice that can only be felt with the heart.

"Nothing can dim the light, which shines from within."
-Maya Angelou

Life presents a number of difficult challenges for all people. As we review our lives, it is important to realize that absolutely nothing has the power to dim the light that shines within, unless you surrender that power to another. Allow your unique inner light to shine brightly, just as it is meant to do.

II

The Sanctuary Within

Modern life is filled with a variety of distractions, activities, duties, concerns, violence, and overstimulation of every kind. All of these, can and often, do contaminate our thoughts, which can launch us into a cycle of anxiety, fear, worry, depression, and swirling mind activity that can be hard to manage.

What can we do about it?

The answer may be simpler than you might think. We are hard-wired for success in our lives, coming into this world with resilience, happiness, and the capability to live fully present in any given moment. We only need to observe young children at play to see how truly present they are. They have no worries about the past or anxiety about the future. Even when they are frustrated or upset, they erupt quickly, and then let the feeling pass, moving on to the next activity, without a single care.

As we move out of early childhood, we slowly begin to allow external circumstances to invade our inner space, bit by bit. One day, we awaken to a mistaken belief that external events have the power to control our inner world. This illusion begins to slowly color every aspect of our lives, unless we realize that this is just a very big misunderstanding.

In reflection and stillness, you can discover a magnificent sanctuary within that contains all of the answers that you have been seeking. Within this inner sanctuary, you can find clarity of understanding and clarity of thought to direct your life. This magical place within is where you can truly be yourself, reunited with the happy being that came into this world seeing, hearing, and feeling absolute wonder about everything. This world of wonder still lives within you and is patiently waiting for you to find your way back home. The happiness you seek is not out there, in the world or hidden from you, by the universe. Happiness is already within you.

"The privilege of a lifetime is being who you are."
-Joseph Campbell

It is a distinct privilege to accept and love yourself, exactly as you are. When you realize that molding yourself into the expectations of others will not bring you lasting peace or happiness, you are free to become who you really are.

"Our anxiety does not come from thinking about the future, but from wanting to control it."
- Kahlil Gibran

Stress and anxiety arise when we place inappropriate focus onto the future. It is not pondering the future or making plans for it that creates anxiety; it is feeling an intense and overwhelming need to control it. Directing our thoughts and attention onto this very moment, right now, will better equip us to deal with the future as it naturally unfolds on its own. We only ever have this very moment, right now.

"Every moment is a moment of decision, and every moment turns us inexorably in the direction of the rest of our lives."
- Mary Balogh

Thoughts determine feelings, with actions, shortly following. While we cannot control what thoughts arise in our mind, we can control the amount of attention that we give to them. If a negative thought is simply ignored, a new thought will quickly rise up to take its place. Choose wisely, the thoughts that you allow to establish deep roots within your mind. Thoughts determine the very direction that your life will take, much more than you can imagine.

"You can chain me, you can torture me, you can even destroy this body, but you will never imprison my mind."
- Mohandas Karamchand Gandhi

The mind is an extremely powerful force and one that we often underestimate. In spite of external circumstances, no matter now heinous they may be, each of us has all of the innate resilience that we need to overcome adversity in its many forms. No one has the power to imprison your mind, unless you surrender yourself to their control.

"When you can't change the direction of the wind, adjust your sails."
- H. Jackson Brown, Jr

When we are passing through threatening ill-winds, rather than fighting them, we simply need to hang on with all of the strength we possess, while we adjust our sails. Storms never last forever. In the aftermath of any storm, comes a peaceful calm. It is within this calm, that you discover who you really are.

"Only a child sees things with perfect clarity because it hasn't developed all those filters which prevent us from seeing things that we don't expect to see."
- Douglas Adams

Take a moment to view the world as a child sees; without filters, without contaminated thoughts, and with a sense of wonder and amazement about everything. As we do this, we make contact with our innate wisdom and find all the resilience that we need to carry on. Life becomes crystal clear, when we seek to view the world through the lens of child-like wonderment.

12

Resilience Comes from Within

Every living being is subject to challenges and obstacles. We either succumb by allowing our thoughts to be poisoned by our circumstances or we can choose to look within us, where we will find all the adaptability and clarity of thought that we need to weather any problems. Here is the thing—in the midst of seemingly insurmountable obstacles, we can only find strength and inner peace by looking inward; the place where our spirit resides. We cannot find peace and comfort in sufficient enough amounts to sustain us by looking *anywhere else*.

The only barrier that may be preventing you from accessing your innate, resilient spirit, is the deafening chatter of your own toxic thoughts. Quiet your mind, by whatever means works for you. Some quiet their mind by sitting on the beach, reflecting on the rhythm of the waves. Others find solace by listening to a waterfall, observing the movement of a river, watching the sunset, contemplating the sounds of nature, taking a walk, listening to peaceful music, or by participating in formal meditation exercises. It is within the context of this stillness, that you may appreciate even the tiniest glimpse of the tremendous inner-strength that you already possess. This inner-strength will gently guide you, toward improved clarity of thought and provide you with insight into your life.

The silent space, within, is where you can discover all of the answers and resilience required to lead you gracefully through any circumstance, no matter how challenging it may be. While external challenges come and go in every person's life, only you hold the power within, to overcome any obstacles in your life.

"When one door closes, another opens; but we often look so long and so regretfully upon the closed door that we do not see the one which has opened for us."
- Alexander Graham Bell

Life is filled with disappointments and closed doors. Insights can appear in the most unlikely places and appear, when we least expect them. When one door closes, look for another opening. An open mind is the conduit for understanding where to look.

"Three things in human life are important. The first is to be kind. The second is to be kind. And the third is to be kind."
- Henry James

While, we may not be able to change the world on a grand scale, we can always refine our view of the world. By changing our perspective, we can touch the lives of those in our immediate surroundings. Acts of kindness will not just change the lives of others. Kindness changes our own experience of life. It is the greatest gift that one can give to another.

"Our life is frittered away by detail...simplify, simplify."
- Henry David Thoreau

What plagues the majority of us is negative, cluttered thinking about a future that has not and may not ever happen. Conversely, we may find ourselves ruminating about a past that we can never, ever change. The simplicity of remaining present in this moment is liberating, allowing incredible insights, and new thoughts to emerge from within us. It is, within silent moments, that positive thoughts can make their way into our awareness.

"No act of kindness, no matter how small, is ever wasted."
- Aesop

In this world filled with uncertainty, hatred, and violent acts, it is easy to feel overwhelmed. An encouraging word, a smile, or an anonymous kind gesture is never wasted. It may make all the difference in a person's life. It certainly can make a tremendous difference in your own life.

13

Your Life Is a Result of Your Choices

Modern society conditions us to believe that the current circumstances of our life are a direct result of the behaviors of others; that external events, somehow, control us. We usually seek someone else to blame, when life does not turn out the way we planned: our parents, our government leaders, our jobs, or events that occurred in the past. There is more than enough blame to go around and it is toxic. What most of us fail to grasp is that to enjoy a better life, we must first learn to make better choices.

Events that may have occurred in the past have no power over us in the present moment.

No matter how horrible events may have been in the past when they occurred, they can either become learning experiences that we store in our memory for future reference, or events that continue to plague us, as we relive them over and over in our mind. How we process these past events is paramount. If we allow external events to shape our present or future state of mind, we experience a life filled with confusion, anxiety, and a sense of constant dread or urgency. Instead of being *reactive* to external circumstances, we have the ability to pause a moment to become centered, then choose to *act wisely*, instead of reacting. By remaining connected with our inner spirit for guidance, we can develop a deeper understanding of the fact that it is our perception of events that creates our experience of our life, not the events themselves.

Life is a result of the choices that we make, moment by moment. While it is true that everyone experiences trials and tribulations in their lives from time to time, it is up to each of us to resist allowing them to defeat us. As we gain a deeper understanding of the *inside-out* nature of life, better choices become instinctive. Clinging to the inside-out nature of life, in the midst of chaos, is our best defense against a lifetime of circumstances.

"Bravery is an ocean in an island of fear. To be brave is not to be fearless; instead, it is to be fearful, yet remain unmoved by that fear."
-Teal

There are many moments in our lives, where we may allow fear to defeat and paralyze us. It is in those moments that bravery seems impossible. Being brave is not being fearless. It is being gripped by fear, while doing what needs to be done anyway. Never doubt that each of us has an innate capacity to be brave, when it is the right thing to do.

"In the middle of every difficulty, lies opportunity."
- Albert Einstein

No matter what may be going on in one's life, underneath the surface lies an opportunity to see things differently. If we stand back and look at life through a wider lens, we can more easily see the shore on the distant horizon, instead of mistakenly believing that we are forever lost at sea.

"I've lived through some terrible things in my life, some, of which, actually happened."
-Mark Twain

The majority of what haunts us, is merely the misguided imaginings of the mind. Once we realize this innocent misunderstanding, we can better appreciate the importance of valiantly and vigilantly protecting the quality of our thoughts as if our lives depend on it; because, in reality, it does.

"Don't let people pull you into their storm.
Pull them into your peace."
-Kimberly Jones

While it is very tempting to react to insults, hateful behaviors, rude gestures, or the vile acts and demeaning speech of people at work, home, or from our political leaders, it is important to resist reacting to them. Instead, pause to look within and become grounded, *before* you speak. Within, is where you will find all of the clarity you need to carefully choose your actions without reaction. Maintaining an inner calm in the face of chaos may just attract those around you to share your peacefulness.

"We see things not as they are, but as we are."
-H.M. Tomlinson

The way we view the world, arises from our own thoughts and perceptions about what is going on around us. If we ever hope to change our world, we must, first, take a very careful look, within, to assess the way we view the world. We see the world through the eyes of who *we* are.

"This above all: to thine own self be true, and it must follow, as the night the day, thou canst not then be false to any man."
-William Shakespeare

While we spend much of our lifetime seeking the approval of others or trying to mold our lives into what others demand of us, it is important to realize that this is the cause of tremendous personal anxiety and suffering. If we embrace and accept our authentic-self, while remaining true to who we really are, we have no need for a false front that can only bring us unhappiness. Be yourself and trust that the right people will come into your life, at the right moment.

14

Fears and Your State of Mind

"Fears are nothing more than a state of mind."
-Napolean Hill

Unless you are being physically attacked, at this very moment, with the need to immediately take action to save your life, realize that nearly all of your fears are self-manufactured, toxic thoughts, about imaginary events that have not yet happened and likely, never will happen. These fears can consume your thoughts, create distractions, and lead to more and more anxiety.

Perseverant thoughts, misplaced attention, and ruminating about fears that are entirely imagined, create physiologic responses in the body, in the same way as a genuine, life-threatening attack can provoke. The physiologic response to fear, is an automatic release of a cascade of hormones and neurotransmitters that can cause a number of health problems, if this pattern becomes a chronic, recurrent state. The immediate physical response to being startled or afraid, releases powerful stimulant hormones, causing specific physical reactions, i.e., heart rate increasing, increased blood pressure, hands trembling, and cortisol hormone release. These symptoms dissipate in about five minutes or less, once the initial threat is over. However, if anxious thoughts are sustained, your physical body will maintain this fearful state and the physical symptoms produced by those thoughts.

It is possible to allow fearful thoughts about what *might* happen in the future, to pass through you, without allowing them to take root, by simply ignoring them. When you do not engage with fearful thoughts, new thoughts will arise quickly to take their place. Direct your attention into the present, to realize that, at *this* moment, you are safe from imminent harm. With your full attention in the present, you are in a much better position to experience promptings from your inner spirit to provide you with direction. Problems cease to be problems when you make this a regular practice, instead of transforming them into situations to navigate.

Everything That You Want, You Are Already That...

Most of the stress and anxiety that we experience in life, comes from the erroneous yet, innocent belief that external circumstances determine our capabilities. We fail to grasp that every living thing arrives into mortality, with an innate, inner compass, hard-wired within them. This innate self-correcting system can always be accessed within the context of silence and a quiet mind. In the silent pause between thoughts, this power is waiting to be recognized. Where there is even a nanosecond of space between the constant barrage of external stimuli and obsessive thoughts swirling about in our brain, insights are there awaiting your discovery.

You possess timeless wisdom within. As you reverently reflect on this ancient power, if only for the briefest of moments, your fears and anxieties will melt away with light and wisdom, arising from within you, to take their place.

"The power is in you. The answer is in you. And you are the answer to all your searches. You are the goal. You are the answer.
It's never outside."
-Eckhart Tolle

When we are very young, we exist in a constant state of wonder, amazement, and live entirely in the moment. We have no concept of past or future. There is only now. Regardless of circumstances around us, we are confident and free. We have to be taught to develop insecurities, self-doubt, anxiety, distrust, hatred, and fear. Look within, to connect with your inner spirit and discover all of the answers you need to direct your life.

"Gratitude is the sign of noble souls."
-Aesop

Being grateful, for what one has, is congruent with our deeper, nobler selves. Instead of worrying about what may come to pass in the future, pining after what we do not have in the present, or lamenting about past experiences, we can be grateful for the life we have at this moment.

"Although the world is full of suffering, it is also full of the overcoming of it."
-Helen Keller

Trials and obstacles are very much a part of living. No one is immune from challenges in their lives, although we may believe that some people are. We don't really know what another person is experiencing, unless we take the time to understand them. Realize that it is not the degree of our suffering that defeats us; it is giving in to desperation. We have tremendous power within, to overcome any challenge.

ᴋness cannot drive out darkness: only light can do that.
Hate cannot drive out hate: only love can do that."
-Martin Luther King, Jr

As circumstances occur in our lives, no matter how dark they may be, we must resist the temptation to sink into despair, or to embrace dark thoughts and hateful feelings about them. Hate can never conquer hate. Only love, light, calm determination, and conducting one's life with the sure rudder of our innate spirit, will conquer darkness and the dark forces around us.

"A man of calm is like a shady tree. People, who need shelter come to it."
-Toba Beta

As uncertainty and anxiety surround us, we can still experience clarity of thought and resilience to manage each situation as it presents itself. Peaceful calm is our natural state. Dig deeply to connect with this inner force and you will not only conquer your life's challenges with dignity, but you will also be poised to provide inspiration to those around you, who need your unique talents to overcome their own struggles.

15

Joy Will Burn Out the Pain

"Find a place inside where there's joy and the joy will burn out the pain."
-Joseph Campbell

In spite of what may be humble beginnings, it is very important to understand that each of us already possesses the capacity to experience joy and happiness in our lives.

Within every being, there is a timeless and formless essence or spirit, that binds us to each other. This powerful force within, has the ability to guide us through any situation and to assist us in achieving happiness in our lives. When we are faced with situations that particularly challenge us, this awesome force can give us specific insights and provide us with the direction we need, moment by moment. We do not need to seek solutions or direction from anyone else. Everything that we need is already within us, waiting to come into our awareness.

Search, within, for this guiding light. It can only be accessed with a quiet mind. Within you, is the only place where pure happiness can be found. Just as light drives out the darkness, happiness can burn away all of your pain.

"If you have inner peace, nobody can force you to be a slave to the outer reality."
-Sri Chinmoy

No matter what horrors, chaos, negativity, or disappointments may be lurking in the world, each of us possesses a haven of peace, within, where no one can dominate or enslave us. Resist being drawn into the negativity of the world around you. Look deeply within to know with absolute certainty that no circumstance or memory from the past, has any power to destroy your inner world, unless you surrender your power.

"Be more concerned with your character than your reputation, because your character is what you really are, while your reputation is merely what others think you are."
-John Wooden

We spend a great deal of our lifetime concerned about what others think about us. This creates a considerable amount of anxiety and suffering. No one will be liked or admired by everyone. What is most important is to develop and align your character with your authentic self, without allowing the world to deposit toxic thoughts into your mind. Your character is who you really are. Being someone that you are not, will never lead to happiness or inner peace. Remember who you really are.

"Calmness is the cradle of power."
-Josiah Gilbert Holland

Accepting what *is*, does not mean that we need to subject ourselves to abuse by others. Quite the opposite. It means that we accept any situation for what it already is, without judgment, viewing the situation unfolding from the vantage point of an astute observer. From within that powerful perspective, we can make better decisions about how we need to act, in that moment, directed by insights arising from within us. The inside-out perspective is not reactive or impulsive. Insight arises from a place of calm; the cradle of tremendous personal power.

"We cannot solve our problems with the same thinking we used, when we created them."
-Albert Einstein

When we rely solely on our intellect to solve problems, we can get into a negative feedback loop that results in the same problems, arising over and over again. What we need, is a new perspective. This does not come from our intellect. A new perspective must arise from insight. All the insight that we need for any situation is already there within us, waiting to surface. Listen intently to the space between breaths, the stillness of nature, the rhythmic lapping of waves on the shore. This stillness is how we receive insights that are trying to gain our attention. Insight can only come to our awareness, when we are not *thinking*.

"Don't become too occupied with what is happening around you; pay more attention to what is going on within you."
-Mary-Frances Winters

We are all subject to unsettling events and circumstances, even though it may appear that we are alone in our trials. No one escapes hardships. What is important, is to remain open and connected to your inner-self, where you can discover the peaceful calm, that exists within *any* storm. We are born with a resilient, powerful, happy, and malleable spirit. This spiritual essence has the capacity to provide us, with the guidance we need, when we need it, at any moment. Look *within* for calm, no matter what may be going on around you. Peaceful calm is never found outside of you. It can only be found within.

"It's not what you look at that matters, it's what you see."
-Henry David Thoreau

How we experience life is entirely dependent on our thoughts and perceptions about it. The thoughts, we focus on, color all of our perceptions of life. Others may look, at the same scene that you are, and yet, see things very, very differently. If you want to see true beauty in the world, happiness within your life, and joy in your relationships, carefully choose the quality of thoughts that you entertain. Rise above your conditioning.

16

Happiness Can Only Be
Found Within You

The purpose of life has been debated by numerous scholars, through-out the ages, all over the globe. We may spend our entire lifetime trying to figure out what our purpose in life really is, as we strive to make our mark in the world. We can find ourselves constantly seeking to be somewhere else, or even someone other than who we already are. In reality, what we are longing for is our *timeless self;* the infinite and unique spirit that resides within each of us, from the very moment that we arrived into this mortal world.

Most of us have forgotten how to remain in contact with our true-self. Life and its many ups and downs has directed our thoughts out-ward, toward the expectations of others. Somewhere along the way, we began to believe that the external world, has tremendous power over who we are. We have become convinced that circumstances or events that may have happened to us in our lives, can actually dictate who we can become, entrapping us in a predetermined mold that cannot be broken. This is an innocent misunderstanding.

We are not doomed to remain an unwilling hostage of the past or to be forever entrapped in a state of anxiety about the uncertainty of the future. All we ever really have, is this present moment. If we learn to accept the power that is inherent within the present moment, we can more easily recognize the resilient and wise spirit within us, that is attempting to gain our attention, which cannot be destroyed, under any circumstances.

As you quiet the constant chatter of your mind and listen intently to the still small voice within, you will find direction and guidance that is far beyond the capability of your personal intellect alone. You may search the world over, looking for someone, some place, or something to 'make you' happy, but true and lasting happiness can only be found within *you*. It is already there, gently calling to you to come home, to who you really are.

"If an egg is broken by an outside force, life ends.
If an egg is broken by an inside force, life begins.
Great things always begin from the inside."
-Jim Kwik

External pressures are present all of the time, regularly attempting to crush our spirit. It is only when we break out of our self-imposed shell, that we can become our authentic self and achieve true greatness. You already have everything you need within you, ready to break free.

"There is a huge amount of freedom that comes to you when you take nothing personally."
-Don Miguel Ruiz

The ego wants to take every action by others, as either a personal complement or a personal insult. Who we really are is much more substantial than our ego alone. There is great freedom in the realization what others may say or do to offend, has absolutely nothing to do with who you are, and has everything to do with who they are. By not interpreting any given behavior by others as a direct personal attack, you retain more personal power than you can even imagine. This understanding allows you to maintain inner calm, peacefulness, and natural protection from any external circumstance, threatening to damage your inner spirit.

"People are just as happy as they make up their minds to be."
-Abraham Lincoln

Happiness does not depend upon circumstances, although we are conditioned to believe that it does. Gaining an understanding that our thought-generated perception of life can only arise from within us, allows us to function with a deeper connection to our inner spirit and make the best decisions that we can. This understanding marks the beginning of freedom, wisdom, and happiness; acceptance of what already is and the power of right now.

"Your best teacher is your last mistake."
– Ralph Nader

While we often beat ourselves up emotionally for making errors in judgment, these missteps are our very best teachers. Know that, each of us is doing the best we can with the understanding of life that we have at the time. As we grow in our understanding of life and how it works, we can learn from our mistakes and choose more wisely the next time.

"It's all about finding the calm in the chaos."
-Donna Karan

We cause a great deal of personal suffering to ourselves, by thinking that we can control circumstances. While we may attempt to control circumstances by choosing a particular course of action with one specific outcome in mind, that is rooted in controlling the future, this only creates reactionary responses, instead of wise actions. This thought-process is often accompanied by a strong sense of urgency and anxiety. Accepting what already *is* and working within it, in a state of calm, empowers you to make the best decisions available for your unique situation, arising from a place of wisdom, instead of fear.

17

The Wizard Behind the Curtain

The human brain is an amazing organ, whose function is to make associations, recognize patterns, project how to avoid painful patterns from the past, recall memories, keep all systems of the body in working order, and create ongoing perceptions of the world around us. While it is a useful servant for maneuvering this life, it is a terrible master. The brain seeks to be busy constantly, which creates distance from the feeling aspect of our nature.

Although every living thing has a brain, the *Mind* or as I like to call it, *the Wizard Behind the Curtain,* is who we really are, at our very core. We are far more than the functions of our brain. By allowing the Wizard to run the show from behind the curtain, we can maintain constant access to the innate wisdom that every living thing possesses, that is far greater than our personal intellect alone. As the brain is busy creating our personal reality and focusing on thoughts about past wounds or future possibilities, this constant activity can distract us from recognizing the inherent power within the present moment. The present is not only the place, where we can find insight to guide us in the moment. The present moment is all that we ever really have.

The past is gone, the future uncertain, while the present is where life unfolds.

When you are very still and able to step away from the feeling of being solely identified by the content of your thoughts, it is in that exact moment that insight can rise up from within you to offer you specific guidance. When your thoughts are in over-drive and your feelings are overwhelming, it is important to understand that 100% of your feelings are coming from your thoughts in that moment, not from any circumstances surrounding you. Feelings are not an accurate predictor of future scenarios and do not have any special residual powers over you from past events. Feelings are merely thoughts in the moment, with feelings attached. We can easily be tricked by our thoughts.

Feelings are a great barometer of current thought *only* and may not have anything at all to do with external circumstances. Feelings represent the thoughts and perceptions that you have *about* events and are not coming directly from the events themselves. In other words, nothing has the power to *make* you feel a certain way. Your feelings are always coming from your thoughts about any given situation, in that moment. By understanding this and not reacting to the constant buzzing of external circumstances around you, you can more easily connect with your inner spirit for guidance and abandon the chaotic feelings that you may be experiencing about circumstances.

See your thoughts for what they are; servants for use when needed, NOT the masters of your destiny. You are far more than any random thought that your brain can generate! You are the Great Wizard Behind the Curtain!

"Two things to remember in life;
take care of your thoughts when you are alone and take care of your
words when you are with people."
-Author unknown

The difference, between a happy life and an unhappy one, depends entirely on the quality of our thoughts. While we cannot control the many thousands of thoughts that pop into our head on any given day, we do have control over which ones we choose to give our attention. It is placing our focus on negative, toxic thoughts that allows them to direct our actions and take over our personal mind. All of our actions begin with a thought. The thoughts we entertain lead to action.

"Sometimes the easiest way to solve a problem is to stop participating in the problem."
-Jonathan Mead

We can easily forget that the solution to many of our problems is to stop participating in the problem. What that means is that when someone is challenging you on an issue, you do not have to justify yourself or your position on the matter. If you pause a moment to reflect on the issue when challenged, this momentary pause, allows you to make contact with your inner spirit, to guide you in how to appropriately respond in that moment. Sometimes, not responding is the best solution. Your inner spirit will let you know the best choice to make, if you listen.

"The quieter you become, the more you can hear."
-Ram Dass

We are constantly bombarded with so much activity in our mind that cluttered thinking can take over our lives, distancing us from who we really are. It is in quiet moments that we are better able to make contact with our inner spirit. Take time each day to reflect for just a few moments, free of distractions and noise. Listen intently to your spirit, as it silently speaks to you without words, guiding you gently toward the best decision that you can make, at any given moment. The answers you seek are already within you.

"Inner peace does not come from getting what we want, but from remembering who we are."
-Marianne Williamson

It will serve us well to remember that inner peace does not come from any circumstances outside of us or from getting everything we want in the material world. Inner peace can be recognized as we develop a sense of who we really are and conduct our lives according to that understanding. Peaceful calm is our timeless and eternal nature.

"Our human compassion binds us the one to the other, not in pity or patronizingly, but as human beings, who have learnt how to turn our common suffering into hope for the future."
-Nelson Mandela

All beings have an innate ability to express compassion for one another.We are bound to one another by our common origin and shared struggles, no matter who we are or where we may live. It is easy to forget that we are all connected, especially when we are caught up in the hustle and bustle of the material world. It is, when we act compassionately toward others, that we are the closest to being our authentic self.

"Knowing yourself is the beginning of wisdom."
-Aristotle

To understand and remain true to yourself, marks the beginning of wisdom. When you are true to yourself, you will never need to change who you are to garner the acceptance of others with lesser ideals. You can stand strong in your convictions and be your own person. This is what you have been seeking your entire lifetime. Your inner spirit is within you, patiently waiting for you to recognize it.

18

Letting Go of Habitual Thought

Our personal mind is constantly sorting and analyzing data that is uploaded through the five senses of sight, sound, touch, taste, and smell. The brain is always 'on', without any 'off' button. Data is collected, patterns recognized, and associations made, while all of this information is collectively interpreted with the prime directive of our survival.

The brain is always seeking something to do.

We are designed to instinctively recognize danger or any imminent threat to our survival. It is not something that usually requires *thinking*. For example, if we see a fast-moving car coming down the road, aimed directly at us as we are crossing the street, it does not require any detailed analysis to leap out of the way to safety. We instinctively have the ability to save ourselves from imminent danger, as part of our hardwiring.

When a 'close call' like this occurs, the brain will remember the incident every time we cross a busy street, reminding us that the same dangerous scenario could recur. If we give that thought our full attention and allow new fearful thoughts to be generated around it by creating mental *what if* scenarios, our physical body will respond automatically with a fight or flight response. Our heart rate will increase, our breathing will become rapid, our pupils will dilate, and we will feel immense fear and panic at the very sight of a car roaring down the street, whether is it coming dangerously close to us or not. This visual image can trigger a powerful recall of memory and put into motion this same physiologic reaction over and over again, only, in this case, based upon memory, not reality.

This is how thought works in everyone. Feelings are a direct reflection of our thinking, in any given moment. Feelings provide immediate feedback about our current thoughts. If we are feeling frightened or panicked, our thoughts are those of fear and panic, in that moment. If we give fearful thoughts additional focus, or attention, fearful feelings grow as the thoughts grow, creating a vicious negative feedback loop in our brain. This is how habitual thought patterns are created and get us 'stuck' in a toxic pattern.

The autonomic function of the brain cannot discriminate between real or imagined danger with its physiologic responses. Whether you merely think that you are in some sort of danger or actually are in imminent danger, the body responds physiologically exactly the same way; with increased *fight or flight* stress hormones; epinephrine, cortisol, norepinephrine, and others. If fearful or anxious thoughts become a chronic state, this chronic overproduction of stress hormones can lead to diabetes, weight gain, cancer, poor sleep, high blood pressure, mental illness, and many other health problems.

The way to let go of these habitual toxic thoughts is to first recognize that they are simply randomly generated thoughts that the brain has created for survival, based upon past associations. If you indeed *are* under direct physical attack, remember that you don't *have* to think. You instinctively act first and think later, in any life-threatening scenario. We are designed to instinctively protect ourselves from present and imminent physical attack, with a well- functioning fight or flight physical response.

Everyone is designed with an instinct for self-preservation.

Pay attention to your thoughts. When you recognize that you are experiencing a fearful thought or feeling, take a couple of deep breaths to slow you down, giving you space to actually assess the current situation accurately. If you are not in any real danger and cannot do anything, at this very moment, to change your situation, accept the situation as it is, without resisting it. As you do, fearful thoughts will pass and new random thoughts will arise to take their place, often in the form of insight on what to do next.

This process works for any thoughts and associated feelings that may arise. By not reacting impulsively to circumstances, you are more easily able to access your inner spirit for guidance, which is always connected to the vast collective wisdom of the Universe. Not lending any meaningful attention to negative thoughts, interrupts the downward spiral toward the creation of even more negativity, *what if* scenarios, and toxic behaviors. Your inner spirit is always present, waiting to direct you, *if* you listen carefully to its promptings. It cannot direct you by force. You must first allow it to work within you, and through you.

In the midst of chaotic circumstances of any kind, whether real or imagined, *pause* to carefully assess the situation. Recognizing destructive, reactive thoughts, in the moment, for what they really are, will help you to avoid the creation of imaginary thoughts, that can take you further away from reality and impede access to your innate wisdom.

Each of us has walked along a beach, stood on a mountain top, sat quietly on a hill overlooking rolling fields, or have laid quietly in our bedroom listening to the pitter patter of raindrops on the window, when suddenly we received an insight or 'aha' moment about what to do to resolve a problem; something that we had not thought of before.

Insight does not come to us when our thoughts are busy over-analyzing about what to do next, especially if it has not yet revealed a simple solution from our intellect alone already. Your Inner Spirit, aka the Universal Mind, has the ability to access the vast collective wisdom at its disposal at any time; wisdom that your *brain*, alone, simply does not have the ability to access. Insight can only be accessed when we are still and reflective. We all possess this amazing gift, although we are often too bogged down within the quagmire of destructive thought to recognize that it is there, patiently attempting to make its way into our consciousness.

While we must rely on our brain and intellect for practical matters in mortal life, the brain must remain subordinate to our inner spirit, if we expect to ever experience lasting happiness. When you conduct your life with direction from your inner spirit, instead of operating from superstitious notions that external circumstances have some sort of power to cause your thoughts or feelings, you are much better equipped to let go of habitual, toxic thoughts that may be sabotaging your life.

While no one has the ability to control circumstances, you do have complete control of your thoughts and feelings about them. Accepting what *is* without resisting, allows you to more effectively deal with any situation, without creating negative emotions and thoughts that can distract you from reality. The practice of accepting what already is and working within it, promotes a calm and peaceful state of well-being. While functioning within this state of calm, you can make better choices, consciously deciding whether to withdraw yourself from the situation, address the situation directly with a measured response, or choose to not take any further action, at this moment.

This is what it means to be conducting your life from the inside-out perspective, which is the only way that life really works. We are designed to function very well in the context of reality. We are not designed to function in an imaginary world that only exists in our brain, that has been created by our toxic thoughts. Living life from an outside-in perspective, as if circumstances have the power to rule or ruin our life and our thinking, is always an illusion.

Illusions destroy our happiness, our relationships, place us in isolation, and prevent us from accessing our inner spirit for guidance. Seeing life as it really is and working within it, instead of against it, allows us

fe without contaminated, habitual thoughts, while
om a higher power within.

"Our job is to love others, without stopping to inquire whether or not t
are worthy."
-Thomas Merton

The most noble act is to love, without judging the worthiness of the recipient. This is the mindset that came with us, when we arrived into this world. It is not often the thinking that we have, when we leave it. Listen carefully to your inner voice. As you do, you will be better equipped to understand how essential love is to all beings; most especially to yourself.

"The greatest weapon against stress is our ability to choose one thought
over another."
-William James

We are conditioned to believe that stress is due to forces outside of our control. With this belief, we surrender ourselves to circumstances. The reality is that, what we believe is causing our stress, is actually our perception of events, not the events themselves. When we conduct our life from an inside-out perspective, instead of the outside-in way of thinking, we are able to realize that the ability to choose one thought over another is the pathway to freedom from any type of stress.

"The glow of one warm thought is to me worth more than money."
-Thomas Jefferson

The power of thought is a tremendous force. Positive, peaceful thoughts allow us to more easily navigate this world. Negative thoughts are usually accompanied by a deep sense of dread and urgency, giving us not only a poor opinion of others, but also of ourselves. We have the power to choose the amount of attention that we give to any given thought.

"Believe in yourself and all that you are. Know that there is something inside of you that is greater than any obstacle."
-Christian D. Larson

We are born with a certainty inside each of us, allowing us to overcome any obstacles in our way. With time, we can allow our thinking to wander off, creating a distance from that certainty. Know that you are greater than any obstacle in your path! It is within moments of silent reflection and calm, that you can reconnect with that certainty and all of the resilience that you will ever need to overcome any adversity.

"If you don't like something, change it; if you can't change it, change the way you think about it."
-Mary Engelbreit

We create a great deal of stressful thinking by not accepting circumstances as they are and working within that reality. While we cannot change what is occurring around us at any moment, accepting the situation for what it is, allows us the ability to access Divine Intelligence. As we do, we are free to thoughtfully choose the right action to take in any situation. You always have the power to change your point of view.

19

Star Wars Lessons

I love the *Star Wars* series, like millions of fans worldwide. I was so excited to see *The Rise of Skywalker* hit the theaters. The movie, certainly, did not disappoint, brilliantly weaving George Lucas' famed characters from Episodes I-VIII, into an exciting adventure with heroes and villains for us to, both, love and despise.

Why do we find the *Star Wars* series so alluring? Is it the action, the science fiction theme, the good vs evil drama unfolding, the family struggles, the theme of betrayal, or is it deeper than all of that?

I find that this particular series has impacted me so profoundly, that I had to search my own feelings to understand *why*. I discovered, that it is the premise of a Force, directing the universe that resonates so deeply with me; the universal nature of our spiritual identity cloaked by a mortal form.

Each of us innately possesses a *Force* within that is far greater than our human form alone. This Force is the true nature of who we really are. There have been many visionaries throughout history, who have touched upon this theme with metaphors of their own, who have successfully built their own following. One of my favorite expressions of this archetypal concept is that of the visionary philosopher, Sydney

Banks, who describes the Three Principles of Mind, Consciousness, and Thought and their relationship to the human experience.

Mind refers to the Universal Mind or, in other words, the innate spirit that each of us possesses that is a part of the greater whole of the spiritual nature of the Universe. This formless Mind binds us one to another and is the source of all wisdom. Each of us arrives into the mortal world with this amazing gift, clothed by a mortal frame. The further we drift away from infancy, the more we distance ourselves from feeling connected to our spiritual nature. Our personal reality can become contaminated with illusions of our own creation, prompted by innocent misunderstanding about who we really are. It is easy to be deceived into misunderstanding; our true identity in this chaotic world of over-stimulation, anxiety, and worry. We may spend our entire lives searching for answers out in the world, while this *something* that we seek so desperately has been within us all along, without our realizing it. The wisdom of the universe is already within us.

Consciousness is the ability to be aware of our surroundings and to make sense of what is happening around us. The fact that we are alive and actually aware that we are alive is the essence of the principle of consciousness.

Thought is the more interesting of these principles and literally creates the world that we perceive as our reality. Thoughts have feelings attached; feelings that are forged by our perceptions of life. The mortal brain processes data gathered from our senses, makes associations from memories, merges them with new events, and attempts to make sense of these collective experiences.

Thought can construct a colorful world of amazing experiences or create a self-imposed, illusory hell that is made up of serial misconceptions. Many of us are mistakenly convinced that our thoughts can magically create the future we want. We can, also, be innocently deceived into believing that past events have powerful dominion over our lives, with lifelong effects that can never be overcome. Neither of these beliefs are true.

These thoughts can be so compelling that we can become absolutely convinced that we can never rise above our past to enjoy happiness in the present or have any hope for our future. We can also become lost in an endless search for something 'out there' to give us the happiness we desire in our relationships, our lovers, our jobs, our family, and from our possessions. This search will always leave us disappointed. Most of us have become so disassociated from our spiritual self that 'out-there' has far more importance to us than the spirit that lives within us. The quest for a meaningful life being discovered in the world outside of ourselves, is an exercise in futility. There is nothing 'Out There' that can ever *make* us happy. Relationships and material things have no magical powers to make anyone happy. It is just not possible.

Each and every being already possesses, within, all that we will ever need to be happy. Everyone possesses a unique portion of the formless Mind that allows us to have insight into *exactly* what we need to do in any given situation. All that is required, to access this tremendous power is to be still and listen.

Everyone has unlimited access to *The Force*, not just the Skywalker family. Every living thing has all of the tools they need to live a meaningful and happy life that is already hard-wired inside of them. It is not possible to be granted the gift of happiness from someone else. This power lies within you alone. While you may benefit from information and support as you discover how to harness your own amazing powers, from an Obi Wan or Yoda instructor, know that you already possess everything that you need to tap into *The Force* within you, at any moment.

Like you, I can, sometimes, allow my intellect and thoughts to trick me. The *Star Wars* allegory reminds me that when I am silent and reflective, freeing my mind of self-created anxieties, the answers I need, will arise powerfully from within me, accompanied by a certainty that is far beyond my intellect.

Capable of both greatness or tremendous evil, *The Force* can be used for good in our lives and those whose lives we touch, or it can be distorted by an illusory, perceptual creation within a tangled web of thoughts that can be used for great harm to ourselves and those around us. How we utilize the Force is our choice alone to make.

It is comforting to me to know with certainty that who we truly are is not based upon our moment to moment thought patterns. Our thoughts are only telling us what our brain is thinking, at any moment in time. Thoughts are always accompanied by feelings that act as a barometer, letting us know what is going on with our thoughts. These thoughts and feelings are products of our brilliant, ever-flowing, computer-like mind. The formless and nameless aspect of who we really are is much deeper and far nobler than the sum total of our random thoughts. Everyone has the capacity to be a *Jedi*.

My hope, for each of us, is that the deeper meaning of this allegory that is so masterfully woven throughout each of the Star Wars' episodes, might be discovered for yourself, even in this most unlikely of places. As you come to realize that you are all that you will ever need, with powers that are within you that you may not have yet discovered, you will be able to transform your life in ways that are far beyond your wildest imaginings.

May the Force be with you!

"Be kind, for everyone you meet is fighting a hard battle."
-Plato

In spite of how things may appear, everyone has challenges that they are facing in life. A kind word or gesture may be all that a person needs to get through it. One never knows the tremendous impact that we can have on one another. Random, compassionate acts of kindness, will find their way back to you, many times over.

"It is not ignorance but knowledge, which is the mother of wonder."
-Joseph Wood Krutch

The more we learn about life, the more easily we can be filled with wonder. It is wonder that can open the door to insight. Make time to be inspired by the many wonders of this mortal world.

"It is not the ship so much as the skillful sailing that assures the prosperous voyage."
-George William Curtis

There is one thing that sets the course our life will take and that is our thoughts. Thoughts become actions, while our actions are a direct reflection of the quality of our thoughts. Allow the winds of positive thoughts to fill your sails. When the fierce whirlwinds of negativity come, drop your sails and allow them to pass. To navigate life in any storm, guard the quality of your thoughts, above all else.

"Your time is limited, so don't waste it living someone else's life."
-Steve Jobs

Regardless of who we are or the circumstances of our birth, each of us possesses an inner wisdom to better navigate this world. If you stop for just a moment to listen to the space between thought and the constant chatter of noise around you, you will be able to feel ancient wisdom, welling up from within you.

"Listen with ears of tolerance. See through the eyes of compassion. Speak with the language of love."
-Rumi

Some of the more important things to understand, in this life, are how to listen with tolerance, see the world with compassion, and speak with the language of love. As children, we instinctively understood this. As our thoughts became contaminated with negativity, our opinion of life changed. Remember who you really are and how you arrived into this world. As you remember, you can genuinely develop compassion for yourself *and* your fellow beings.

"Mind is the master weaver, both, of the inner garment of character and the outer garment of circumstance, and that, as they may have hitherto woven in ignorance and pain they may, now, weave in enlightenment and happiness."
-James Allen

What we allow to settle into our thoughts, acts like a drop of dye in a bucket. It spreads and colors everything that it touches. The more negativity that we focus on, the more it contaminates and clouds the entire mind. When we focus on positive thoughts and begin to observe negativity without engaging, the mind becomes clearer and our inner-self is preserved. Allow negativity to pass through you, unnoticed.

20

What Causes Our Unhappiness?

Unhappiness is part of everyone's life. When unhappiness washes over us, we usually look around and attribute blame to the present situation that we are in as the direct cause of it. Most of us look to our environment or our circumstances in life, as the cause of our feelings.

Life is never an outside-in experience, although it may seem to be.

Feelings can only arise from within us, never from outside of us. They are an excellent indicator about our thoughts, at the moment. To suppose that events occurring around us have some type of magical powers that can cause us to think a certain way or to feel certain feelings, is very flawed thinking. If we maintain that way of thinking, we will always be tricked into believing that circumstances, events, or people have the power to control us and our emotions. While we cannot control circumstances around us or the behaviors of others, it is completely within our power to determine how we *feel* about those events.

While we may be subject to the rantings and ravings of an angry person, the infidelities of a trusted partner, abuse by a political tyrant, mistreatment in our jobs or by others in a higher social class, or subjected to physical harm and other cruelties, it is important to realize that no one and nothing has the power to ever make us feel a certain way or has the ability to crush our spirit, *unless* we allow it.

We always have the power to look at any situation objectively and allow negativity to pass through us, without offering it a place to roost. While we often hear and may even say, "That makes me so angry," this is never the truth. What we are feeling, is our thoughts about our perception of what just occurred. Again, no situation, person, place, or thing has the power to create feelings in anyone.

It is crucial to understand this.

If we can accept the principle that situations have no power over what we think or feel, we can allow any negative thoughts about a situation to pass through us, far more easily. It is when we endorse negative thinking about any given event or allow negative feelings to fester to the degree that they dominate our mind, that our inner spirit can become profoundly and negatively impacted. It is not any particular situation that has power to wound us. It is our thoughts about the situation that can take control over our happiness.

Our thinking about events is the cause of our unhappiness.

We can choose to see things as they really are and accept what already is as an astute observer. We cannot change what already *is*. That does not mean that we have to allow ourselves to be abused, defeated, or berated. We can accept the present circumstances as they already are and not fight against them. By accepting what is, our mind is free and clear to choose a course of action, guided by our resilient and wise inner spirit. We can choose to flee if we are in imminent physical danger, stand our ground with an appropriate response, walk away to respond later, or simply allow the situation to be, as it passes through us like the wind passing through the branches of a tree. In this way, we remain a wise master of our own thoughts and feelings, instead of allowing circumstances, outside of us, to batter us about.

Our thoughts and feelings *always* arise from within us and are never *caused* by circumstances surrounding us. If we are in touch with what is going on inside of us, we can take appropriate action to protect ourselves from anything that may be going on outside of us. The most important thing that we can do is to realize that circumstances *never* have any power to create unhappiness. The power to create happiness is always an inside job that may be posing as an external imposter. Regardless of anything going on around you, happiness and inner peace can only originate from within us.

You have absolute power to protect what is going on inside of you from anything that is going on outside of you.

"*Happiness is not in our circumstance but in ourselves. It is not something we see, like a rainbow, or feel, like the heat of a fire. Happiness is something we are.*"
-John B. Sheerin

True happiness cannot be found outside of ourselves. We may experience momentary pleasure in material things or relationships, but without being firmly grounded by acceptance and true love of self; the place where happiness resides, these moments are only fleeting, leaving us wanting more. Being true to yourself and continually connected to the wisdom that came with you, as you arrived into this world, is the place where true happiness can be found.

"Wonder is the beginning of wisdom."
-Socrates

We can learn so much about our authentic nature, by observing very young children at play. They live each moment in awe of the ordinary. Experiencing the world around us with awe, wonder, and reverence, marks the beginning of wisdom.

"Feelings are just visitors, let them come and go."
-Mooji

It is easy to be tricked by our feelings. Feelings are a snapshot of our thoughts, at any given moment. Since feelings are connected to fleeting thoughts that randomly arise thousands of times a day, they do not have any real significance, other than they are a reflection of our current thoughts in any given moment. Recognize feelings for what they are, while allowing negative feelings to fall away without engaging them in any meaningful way. New thoughts with new associated feelings will quickly arise to take their place.

"Peace is the result of retraining your mind to process life as it is, rather than as you think it should be."
-Wayne W. Dyer

Most of what actually causes us direct suffering is a misunderstanding of life. Instead of seeing life around us as it is, we view life as how we think it should be. This creates negative thoughts and judgments that only reinforce the notion that if we could only have life as we think it should be, then we could be happy. Accepting what already is and working with it, without judgment, allows us to make better choices with insightful action, instead of impulsive, toxic reactions.

"Don't forget to love her. The little girl you used to be.
Perhaps, she lies within you. Untucked. Sleeping peacefully."
-Kiana Llanos

We are born with an innate resilience and capacity for all of the insight that we need to direct our lives. As young children, we lived entirely in the present, without sadness about the past or worry about the future. In time, our thoughts became distorted, as we distanced ourselves from who we really are. The inner guidance system that we came with into this world, can become buried by layer upon layer of toxic thoughts. In the context of stillness and reflection, rediscover how to love and accept the innocent child that still lives within you, tucked safely away from harm. She is waiting for you to set her free.

21

Open Your Heart

Millions of people of all faiths, races, creeds, and philosophies have spent most of their adult lives endlessly searching for the path that will lead them to happiness. We may follow one path for a while, then become disillusioned as time passes. Restlessness may lead us to another path, then another, and another.

Perhaps, we have stayed on the same path for most of our lives, then one day realize that the answers provided by that way of thinking are at odds with how we actually feel about life. Others may continue in a particular path and not question it, but are left feeling empty inside, blaming themselves for not being *good enough* or *faithful enough*. There are others, who may have been severely wounded by people walking in the same path that they have chosen and are left feeling deeply betrayed, in the life they have chosen.

The quest outside of ourselves for the right path is infinite and ultimately, leads to unhappiness and frustration.

The reason for this deep longing and unsatisfying quest is that we are looking for someone or something to fill the void that exists from being separated from our spiritual self, which has become long forgotten to us, by our mortal self.

The truth is, we are not broken and never need to be fixed, saved, or healed by anyone.

Each of us carries within us a unique piece of the Universe that is seeking to express itself in mortality. This wonderful gift lives within each and every living being. We do not have to earn it or follow a specific path or doctrine to have the right to possess it. It is already ours from the moment we arrive into this world.

The truth we have been searching for is already within us. There is no need to travel anywhere to find truth.

By opening our hearts and emptying our minds of toxic thoughts, the path we need to walk upon will well up from within us and come to our consciousness, when we are ready to recognize it. The meaning of life is already within us. It is when we look outside of ourselves for answers that we can become deceived, frustrated, and left feeling an intense loneliness and longing. The longing that we are feeling arises from being disconnected from who we really are; a spiritual being with all the resilience and clarity that we need to maneuver this earthly plane, under any circumstances. Our inner spirit is within; patiently waiting for us to recognize that it has been there all along. I challenge you to listen carefully to what you may be feeling right now.

Feelings are a direct reflection of our thoughts. If we lend too much attention to thoughts that steer us into a world of toxic imaginations, we distance ourselves from the spirit that lives within us. If we listen carefully to the spirit inside of us speaking to us without words, we can understand the mysteries of the universe, with all the direction we need.

When you are very still and receptive to listening, feeling, and seeing what your inner-self has to reveal to you, you can begin to understand exactly what you need to do in this moment, the next, and the next after that, with an unspoken knowledge that is certain. This clarity of understanding is your inner spirit, speaking to you with the vast wisdom of the Universe at its disposal, gently pointing you in the direction that is right for you.

Resist surrendering your life and your well-being to anyone else. The answers for *your* life are already inside of you. While it is nice to learn about other ideas and gain knowledge about practical matters, it is only the essence of who you are, your inner spirit, that has specific answers for *your* life.

Trust in this process and you will never feel the need to look anywhere else to find happiness.

"The true measure of your character is what you do when nobody's watching."
-Charles Caleb Colton

Character is who you really are, when no one else is looking and when you have nothing to gain. Reputation is what others think of you and is a very illusory thing. This week's top celebrity is next week's old news. Refining your character is what makes the most difference in your life. Surrendering your character to seek the opinions of others is a guarantee for extreme sadness, sorrow, and suffering.

"Authentic power is building something inside of you, which you cannot lose and that no one can take from you."
-Gary Zukav

You have tremendous power within. This power provides all the wisdom and guidance that you will ever need to live a happy life. It cannot be lost or taken from you. While you may temporarily lose contact with this power as you take a few winding turns throughout your life, this power is always there in the wings waiting for you to recognize it. It is your personal compass to guide you, throughout your entire life and in any circumstance.

"Sometimes the most important thing in a whole day is the rest we take between two deep breaths."
-Etsy Hillesum

When your day is busy and your thoughts are buzzing about how to accomplish your daily goals, the most important thing you can do, at that moment, is to fall out of that noisy level of mind activity. Take a few slow, deep breaths, then exhale very slowly to slow down your physical body and calm your thoughts. The space between breaths is where you can experience insight. This space is where you can always come to feel peace amid chaos and receive direction about what is important and what is not.

"At the center of your being, you have the answer, you know who you are and you know what you want."
-Lao Tzu

If you make time for quiet reflection, you can regularly visit that sacred place, within, where your spiritual self resides. It is in moments of stillness when your mind is calm, that you can feel this powerful force rising up from the depths of your soul. This sacred place is where you can understand with certainty, who you really are and what it is that you really want.

"A single twig breaks, but the bundle of twigs is strong."
-Tecumseh

It may seem that people who look different, wear different clothing, or live in other countries are not like us, so they cannot be trusted. The reality is that each of us, no matter who we are, where we live, or how we look, arises from the same spiritual origin. Each of us is innately privileged to receive immeasurable wisdom. We are one earthly family, including all creatures, great and small, who walk among us. Together we are strong; alone we are easily broken.

22

Follow Your Own Path

We may find ourselves blindly following a specific leader, hoping beyond hope that they can shed light on the direction that *our* life ought to take. We see their successes, model after them, and begin to strongly desire the life that they have. However, the more familiar we become with our leader, the more we grow to understand that our golden idol may actually have clay feet. Our hope for some kind of direction becomes dashed. Ultimately, we feel discouraged and betrayed by our revered leader.

Off we go to find another mentor, then another and another, each ending with the same result. Each of our idols is imperfect and guaranteed to disappoint. We, may, go for years basking in the light of one particular guru or spiritual leader or another, but each one will eventually demonstrate to us their imperfections, ending our tightly held fantasy of finding the perfect road to happiness from someone else.

What we are failing to understand is that, each of us has our own distinct path to follow. What may work for one person, may not work for another. Each person is following their own dreams, ideas, and inner light.

*One simply cannot under-estimate the tremendous power that each person
possesses, within them, to guide their own life.*

Insights can only come from within, never from outside of us or
dictated to us from someone else. Insight is an inside experience. As you
listen carefully to your inner voice attempting to gain your attention,
you will be led toward a direction that is right for *you*, not in the direction of a path that is right for anyone else. While others may inspire
you through sharing their personal journey with you, to reach your full
potential listen carefully to your *own* inner voice. This is not only true
in our personal lives. It is also the way to conduct one's professional or
business life. Of course, we need to learn about practical matters, by
acquiring specific training for our professions and businesses, as well
as learning specific skills to function in any given society. Where we
can go astray is by *exclusively* listening to the advice of others and not
listening intently to our own inner voice that is instructing us in how
to *apply* the knowledge and skills that we have learned, for our own
unique situation.

Detailed techniques may work for the instructor with their specific
business and customer base, but a host of dutiful followers are often
sorely disappointed, when they do not get the same replicated results
promised by their leader and mentor in their own businesses. It is crucial to listen to your own unique insights, as you approach every aspect
of your life, even when dealing with practical matters. These insights
will let you know exactly *how* or even *if* to apply any new knowledge
that you have gained, in any particular situation.

Make time, each day, to be very still for a just a few moments,
free from distractions and noise. Many people find that sitting quietly,
while observing nature or listening to soothing music without lyrics (as
lyrics can act as a distraction), can bring them into a space where they
can have meaningful contact with their inner spirit.

Each of us is an integral part of a vast and ponderous whole. No one
is any more privileged than anyone else at accessing this tremendous
gift of spiritual intelligence; the essence of who we truly are. Some may

have more frequent contact with this intelligence than you may have at this point in your journey, but the process for experiencing a powerful connection with your inner-self is the same for everyone. It is literally a single thought away.

The answers you have been seeking throughout your life, have been inside you all along. Pay close attention, as you turn your focus inward. This is where you can find your own guiding light to lead you every step of the way. The world is waiting for what only *you* can contribute to it.

"Kind words can be short and easy to speak but their echoes are truly endless."
-Mother Theresa

The physical world has become very deficient in kind words and deeds.A kind word or a random, anonymous act of kindness can go a very long way in transforming our world into a paradise for all of its inhabitants.

"Until you have real compassion, you cannot recognize love."
-Bob Thurman

Compassion is a trait that is not exclusive to human beings. Compassion is the essence of our true nature. It is also a quality that is inherent in the animal kingdom. We can witness many types of compassionate acts in nature, if we take the time to look. Most truly compassionate acts are those that are performed silently and anonymously. It is the ordinary, everyday acts of compassion, that bind us together as one earthly family.

"A part of kindness consists in loving people more than they deserve."
-Joseph Joubert

Bitter, hateful people usually expect to receive the same treatment that they dish out to others. It feeds their view of the world, as one that is broken. If you observe hateful acts without reacting to them, or allowing the toxic words and deeds that you may be hearing or seeing to enter your inner sanctum, you can maintain your inner peace. Maintaining the sanctity of your inner spirit, allows you to respond to hateful acts, with words and deeds of kindness. It is not a sign of weakness to be kind. Kindness is a noble trait that each of us has the capacity to experience. It is especially needed by those, who deserve it the least, but need it the most.

"A healthy mind observes and questions itself. This is the path to inner peace and happiness. Don't believe everything you think."
-Vironika Tugaleva

Our personal mind is an amazing machine, organizing and analyzing data 24 hours a day, 7 days a week. It is also a master of creating illusions that can steer us away from our true identity and away from reality. We are so much more than our personal mind! We have a unique, spiritual identity that occupies our physical body and a human brain that serves us best as our servant, not as our master. When we focus our attention on a specific negative thought that may arise, we are distracted from our true nature as loving, kind, and happy beings. Don't believe everything you think! The majority of our thoughts are illusions, created by the imaginings of the human mind.

"You must live in the present, launch yourself on every wave, find your eternity in each moment. Fools stand on their island of opportunities and look toward another land. There is no other land; there is no other life than this."
-Henry David Thoreau

We miss out on so much in life by constantly seeking to be somewhere else, looking to be anywhere, other than where we are in this very moment. By doing so, we fail to realize that the best moment of our lifetime is the moment that we are in right now. It is the only moment that we have. The past is a memory, the future a dream. Right now, is the only time, where life and opportunity exist.

"Never be afraid to raise your voice for honesty and truth and compassion, against injustice and lying and greed. If people all over the world... would do this, it would change the earth."
-William Faulkner

No matter who we are or where we live, each of us can courageously stand up for our fellow beings, who may be in harm's way. We are always stronger, when working with others for the common good. To turn away from assisting others, who are being abused or demeaned, is participating in the abuse. As we express compassion and embrace our true loving nature, the world around us can change.

23

Don't Take It Personally

When things go wrong in any relationship, our inclination is to allow the ego to take over our emotions and blame the other person for our feelings, as well as the ultimate demise of the relationship.

How could he (she) do that to me?

Eckhart Tolle, author of *The Power of Now*, describes how to avoid taking things personally, as a strategy to eliminate suffering in relationships of any kind. Letting go of the past, eliminating worry and anxiety about the future, and placing our attention in the present moment, will allow us to have insight, as each moment unfolds.

By not taking things personally, we no longer feel utterly devastated by the constant bombardment of issues arising in life, that may be swirling around us or negatively affected by the unhealthy behaviors of others.

Don Miguel Ruiz, author of *The Four Agreements*, succinctly describes how taking personally the opinions and judgments of others' perceptions of you, can destroy your spirit. By not taking anything personally, we realize that the statements of others, even loved ones, really do not matter in the final analysis. This revelation allows us the freedom to be ourselves and to keep our inner spirit, calm. What matters most is how *you* feel about yourself. When your relationship with yourself is grounded, the relationships you have with others will be healthy and insightful. We simply cannot love anyone else enough to sustain a lasting relationship, without first loving ourselves.

"Individually, we are one drop. Together, we are an ocean."
-Ryunosuke Satoro

As we remain connected with our innate wisdom, we begin to see the world for what it is; one family, one people, intertwined with one another, having arisen from the same universal and magnificent source of wisdom.

"One of the happiest moments in life is when you find the courage to let go of what you can't change."
-Robert Tew

Letting go of attempting to control what you cannot change is not surrendering to apathy. It is acceptance of the realization that you simply cannot control circumstances surrounding you. This insight frees you to more easily maintain inner-calm and serenity, in times of adversity. No matter what may be going on around you, as you increase your inner strength and tap into your resilient nature, you can more easily deal with *any* situation, at any moment. Work with what already *is*, without railing against it, to find solutions for any challenge.

*"If we have no peace, it is because
we have forgotten that we belong to each other."*
-Mother Theresa

We are all beings, who have arisen from the same universal essence. Each of us is equally as important and vital as anyone else. Remember who you really are and it will become easier to understand, that we are all connected, one to another. We are in this mortal life to be happy. It does not really matter how we look, who we choose to love, or where we live. We are all one spiritual family, seeking to experience happiness.

"When you observe rather than react, you reclaim your power."
-Denise Linn

Observing, then calmly choosing how to act is very different from being swept up by external circumstances and reacting to them out of unchecked emotion. Observing without judging, frees you to choose wisely from a place of calm and inner peace. Within you is the place where you have access to the wisdom of the universe.

"Inner peace begins the moment you choose not to allow another person or event to control your emotions."
-Pema Chodron

We are bombarded daily with news of tragic events and acts of hatred on all fronts. It is easy to forget, that none of these events has any real power to control your inner peace, *unless* you allow them to take you over. Be very still and listen intently to connect with your inner-self, to find all the direction you need, even when the world around you is in utter chaos.

24

How to Enjoy a Loving
Relationship

Understanding that external circumstances and superstitious thinking are *not* the source of your well-being, is central to enjoying a loving
relationship with anyone. This is true not only in your relationship
with others, but is especially true in the most important relationship
that you will have in your entire lifetime; the relationship you have
with yourself.

What does that mean?

If you believe that external circumstances and the random behaviors
of others are what actually creates your happiness, or alternately, are the
source of your misery; or if you believe the *"you make me happy"* or *"you
make me sad"* way of thinking about others, then all of your relationships will be filled with misunderstanding, co-dependency, unrealized
expectation, and hurt. Arriving at the realization that your experiences
are a direct result of your *own* feelings, changes *everything* about how
you view the world and your place within it.

As you shift your thinking toward this broader understanding of life, relationships can begin to flourish, accompanied by deepening feelings of love that are free of blame, fault-finding, and the superstitious notion that external forces are in control of your feelings and happiness.

To connect with and love yourself completely with all of your imperfections and gifts, sets the tone for loving others. Without this understanding of self and the innate source of power that you possess, one simply cannot sustain a meaningful relationship with anyone else. Loving acceptance of self, predicates any healthy relationship and its longevity.

When relationships in your life are breaking down, first look to yourself and how you perceive the other person, instead of looking at them to blame for the problem. Are we expecting the other person to somehow magically provide happiness to us? Does anyone really have that power or role? Shifting our view of the other person creates a deeper, reality-based connection.

We are responsible for our own happiness.

We are far more than the sum total of our imperfections, flaws, and behaviors. If you can see beyond the actions of another and are able to connect with the spirit within them, relationships become less strained and more impactful. This does not mean that we can have a close relationship with everyone we meet. We cannot control the feelings and behaviors of others, even if we are accepting and loving toward them. However, you *can* control how you view and treat the other person, choosing to act with loving acceptance, instead of reacting with competitiveness and vengeance.

If you align yourself with others, who also understand the nature of the inner light that resides within them, you will find that these relationships can deepen more easily. Not everyone in our sphere will understand who they really are. All that we can do is accept them, love them, and see in them what they may not yet see in themselves. As you begin to view the world with this lens of clarity, you will be uplifted in ways that you cannot even imagine. This positive light will shine upon each of the lives that come into contact with your spirit.

Realize deeply, that you are never alone. We are all connected to one another spiritually. Whether we realize or accept this truth or not, does not negate its veracity. Each of us possesses a unique piece of the universe within, that links one spirit to another. This understanding opens the door to fulfillment and happiness in our relationships that can span a lifetime.

"Small lights have a way of being seen in a dark world."
-Neil A. Maxwell

In these deeply troubling and chaotic times, that are cloaking the world in misunderstanding, hatred, and negative reactions, even the tiniest spark of love, understanding, or compassion can shed light onto who we really are at our core. We are all connected to the same source of light, whether or not we understand the tremendous power contained within that knowledge.

"We can never obtain peace in the outer world, until we make peace with ourselves."
-Dalai Lama

Peace can only be achieved by first being at peace with ourselves. It does not come to us by force, by calling out differences, through military interventions, or from any type of hateful or violent action. It begins with inner peace and ends with the realization that we are all connected to each other, having arisen from the same creative force. Those, who understand this principle, are the peacemakers in the world.

"Hope is being able to see that there is light, despite all of the darkness."
-Desmond Tutu

Hope is a powerful thing. When all there seems to be is darkness, close your eyes and become very still, directing your attention inward. Within you, is where light can be found, to illuminate your world and dispel all darkness. The eternal light of hope resides within you.

"I did then, what I knew how to do. Now that I know better, I do better."
-Maya Angelou

It is vital to understand that each of us has done the very best we could, with the knowledge and limited understanding that we had at the time. This is a very important concept to understand. This lays the foundation for forgiveness of ourselves, then others.

"Paradise is not a place; it's a state of consciousness."
-Sri Chinmoy

Paradise is freedom from toxic thoughts, not a particular destination. Children are masters at living fully in the present. For them, every moment is paradise. As adults, we forget the exhilarating feeling of wonder, that we possessed in our youth. If we can allow negative thoughts to pass us by, without giving them focused attention, we have space available in our consciousness for positive thoughts and insight. It is within the context of positive consciousness, that we can find our own paradise.

"When you look deeply into your anger, you will see that the person you call your enemy, is also suffering. As soon as you see that, the capacity for accepting and having compassion for them is there."
-Thich Nhat Hanh

Reflect carefully on your feelings of anger, as you gaze intently into the eyes of the person, for whom you are feeling anger or rage. Look beyond their behaviors and into their soul. By doing this, you will be better able to understand that they too, are suffering in ways that you have not yet understood.

25

It's What You See That Matters

"It's not what you look at that matters, it's what you see."
-Henry David Thoreau

How each of us experiences life is entirely dependent on our individual thoughts and perceptions. The thoughts we choose to focus on, color everything about the way we perceive any given situation. We can look at the same scenario as others and yet, still see things very differently from everyone else. Most of us become caught up in the ego's strong desire to be heard and always be *right*, while sacrificing the feelings of those we love and admire. This argumentative and hurtful way of managing differences in our interpersonal relationships, creates distance, lack of intimacy, and ultimately, leads to failure of the relationship.

What can I do to improve conflict resolution within my relationships?

• When challenged, take a moment to pause before saying or doing anything. Reflect on what your loved one is *really* saying and listen for the feelings behind the words. Pause before you speak.

- Choose carefully, at least, one thing that you can say that will show respect for the opinion of the other person, while calmly stating how and why you feel differently.
- Let the other person know that you care for them and value all of their opinions, even if they are different from yours.
- Find, at least, one common idea within the situation that will bring you closer together. You will need to take a moment to step back and objectively ask yourself, *"What in this situation can we agree upon?"*
- End any disagreement with words of love, compassion, and respect.
- Realize that we can all respectfully have and express different opinions and that it is okay to do so.
- Ponder this: Is it worth it to be *right* and to control the opinions of everyone or would it be more beneficial for our relationships to demonstrate respect, empathy, and unconditional love?

If you truly desire beauty in the world around you, authentic happiness, and pure joy in your relationships; be mindful of the feelings of others, while carefully selecting the thoughts that you choose to nurture. Thoughts are accompanied by feelings, while feelings lead to action. Toxic thoughts produce toxic feelings and actions. Positive and loving thoughts produce loving, positive feelings, and respectful actions.

"You can't stop the waves, but you can learn to surf."
-Joseph Goldstein

The ebb and flow of circumstances in life are beyond our control. Everyone is subject to conditions in life that they did not choose. As wave after wave of trials come crashing our way, to arrive safely to shore, learn to ride the waves, instead of fighting them. Accept what already IS.

"Abuse no one and no thing, for abuse turns the wise to fools and robs the spirit of its vision."
-Tecumseh

In a world where we have many choices, we can always choose to be kind. Violence and abuse only perpetuate more of the same and rob us of our true nature.

"Accept – then act. Whatever the present moment contains, accept it as if you had chosen it. Always work with it, not against it."
-Eckhart Tolle

We cannot choose the external circumstances that come and go in our life. We *can* choose how they affect our inner well-being. If we accept what already *is*, we are far more capable of acting, without *reacting*. It is resisting what already *is* and reacting negatively with an internal temper tantrum that creates suffering and unhappiness. Accept; then act, *wisely*.

"Your heart knows the way. Run in that direction."
-Rumi

Your heart, inner spirit, is the essence of who you really are. It knows the direction to take and can light the way for you step by step, as you heed its gentle promptings. Feelings of certainty and calm will well up within you, as your inner spirit is speaking to you. Feelings arising from mortal intelligence alone are uncertain and conflicted. Listen very carefully and you can know the difference.

"Quiet the mind and the soul will speak."
-Ma Jaya Sati

We spend a tremendous amount of energy looking outside of ourselves to find happiness and fulfillment. This search cannot result in what we are seeking. Lasting happiness can only be found within. Listen to the whisperings of your authentic self, gently nudging you, moment by moment, toward the truth you seek.

26

How to Disagree Agreeably

"Conflict cannot survive, without your participation."
-Wayne Dyer

Every relationship has moments when disagreements arise. Some relationships are more laden with disagreements than others.

What can you do when your partner supports a political philosophy or candidate that is the polar opposite of your own philosophy?

How do you reconcile different religious beliefs among family members?

How can you work for a boss, who treats you and your co-workers, disrespectfully?

How do you come to terms with your partner about how to discipline your children?

How do you co-parent your children with an ex-partner, without fighting constantly?

These scenarios represent just a few of the more challenging, ones that life can throw at us. No matter what the conflict may be, the same strategies and 'rules of engagement' can apply in any type of relationship. Here are a few strategies that may be helpful in any disagreement or conflict. Agreeing to disagree; agreeably, is an important skill to learn and one that must be rooted, in respect it to be successful.

Take a few deep breaths.

Taking a moment to breathe deeply will give you a little space to feel your emotions, without reacting to them. It will also help to slow down the body's physical response to perceived stress and conflict, diminishing the fight or flight response; lowering your heart rate and blood pressure for example. Remember, while you cannot control your thoughts and associated feelings, you *can* control how you respond to them. How you choose to act is always a conscious choice. It is important to *act* calmly, while *not reacting* harshly. Pause a moment, then step back to see the bigger picture. It is always best to give a calm, delayed response than to counter-attack, immediately with harsh, cutting words.

It is not personal.

When someone is angry or vehemently disagreeing with you, it is more of a reflection of their own perceptions about life than it is about you. They may be projecting prior hurts, disappointments, and rejections onto you that are not based in the reality of the moment. You are only responsible for your own emotions, not theirs, no matter what their perception may be. It is not about you.

Connect with the person in a meaningful way.

Behind hateful or hurtful words, there is a person with feelings. If they are a loved one, partner, or your child, remember, above all else, that you love them. Looking into their eyes will help you to connect with them and see beyond their hurt in that moment. If appropriate, a gentle touch or pat on the arm or in a work setting, perhaps a hand-shake, can help you to connect with them on a human level.

Clarify.

Ask the person to clarify exactly what the issue is, as they see it. Calmly repeat your understanding of what they just said in your own words. For example, *"What I am understanding is that you feel {repeating what they said}...is that right?"*

Share your feelings without attempting to persuade.

Letting the person know where you are coming from, without trying to persuade them that you are right, will create less resistance and more movement toward common ground.

Treat the person in the way that you would like to be treated.

Would you like someone to bully, persuade, or discredit you, when you disagree with them? Be respectful and try to walk in their shoes for just a moment. It will be easier to understand their position, if you listen with empathy, without judgment.

Look for common ground and build a solution.

If you either step back to see the bigger picture or move in to see closer details, there is almost always some common ground, in which, both parties can agree. You must be willing to shift your view to find it.

Realize that everyone is doing the best they can with their current level of understanding.

While others may have a different understanding than you do, they are doing the best they can, with the limited knowledge that they currently have, no matter how dysfunctional or hurtful it may be. Those with limited knowledge often resist you, out of feelings of insecurity. To find common ground, you must speak to them at *their* level of understanding, not yours.

Let things settle.

Sometimes, planting seeds with more information or a different view point is all that you can do. Although the person may reject your views right now, they may open their mind to new information at a later time. Wait to see what grows. You may be surprised at the results down the road.

Respectfully agree to disagree.

Assure the person that you respect them and that it is okay to not agree on everything. Keep in mind that if their position on an issue is one that your moral compass cannot abide, it may be best to withdraw yourself entirely from the company of that person. Sometimes, removing yourself for your own physical and emotional safety is all that you can do. That is okay, too. It is better to be alone and safe, than to go down an emotionally dark path alongside someone with toxic behaviors.

Remember, the relationship that you have with your inner self is the most important relationship of your lifetime and the one that determines the outcome of all others. If you nurture the relationship that you have with yourself, all of your other relationships will come into sharper focus. The right people will be drawn to you, once you know, accept, and love yourself.

"Happiness is your nature. It is not wrong to desire it. What is wrong is seeking it outside, when it is inside."
-Ramana Maharshi

Looking outside of ourselves to find happiness and fulfillment is a frustrating search that cannot result in what we are seeking. True happiness is not a gift that one can give to another. Happiness can only be found within.

"Surrender to what is. Let go of what was. Have faith in what will be."
-Sonia Ricotti

Not resisting what already is, allows us to remain in the present and to be in touch with our deeper self. Wisdom is conveyed to us from the still, small voice within us, quietly guiding us toward the best decisions that we can make at any given moment. It is not born of this mortal world and is always connected with Universal Knowledge. If we listen carefully to its promptings, we can make better choices than we could ever conjure up using the limited abilities of our personal mind alone.

"Listen to the wind, it talks. Listen to the silence, it speaks.
Listen to your heart, it knows."
-Native American Proverb

It is in the setting of stillness and reflection that you can hear your inner-self speaking. In the space between breaths, is where the wisdom of the ages can be discovered.

"We are not human beings having a spiritual experience. We are spiritual
beings having a human experience."
-Pierre Tielhard de Chardin

To know yourself in the truest sense, is the most important concept to understand in your entire lifetime. We are spiritual beings living in a physical world, not earthly beings in need of a spiritual world. We already *are* spiritual beings. Mortality can distract us from our true spiritual identity, deceiving us into temporarily losing contact with who we really are. We are spiritual beings experiencing mortality.

"The best way to get people to think outside the box is not to create the box
in the first place."
-Martin Cooper

So much of our thinking is habitual, layered with associated rules, restrictions, and fantasy thinking that is not reality-based. This can get us stuck in a negative feedback loop that can be very destructive. While thinking 'outside the box' is certainly an upgrade to narrow-minded thinking, the best approach is to get rid of the 'box' entirely. Open your mind and listen to the spirit within you, where there are no limits.

27

The Hidden Beauty of Adversity

Adversity is not something that anyone seeks or wants to experience in their lifetime. We are usually seeking quite the opposite. Hardships, misfortune, loss of income, divorce, natural disasters, loss of a loved one—these are all experiences that we would like to avoid at all costs.

Most of us would rather bask in the glorious sunlight of prosperity, love, friendship, solid relationships, happy children, a fulfilling work life, and peaceful surroundings. Maybe even a few dollars in the bank for a rainy day. Perhaps, even a vacation home in an exotic location, a high-performance sports car, or a yacht...

Nobody wants to experience adversity!

But what if adversity could actually be helpful for you? The reality of life is, that each and every being experiences challenges and some form of adversity. The role of adversity is to learn how to weather challenges, while remaining true to your inner wisdom; your life compass. As we learn to overcome challenges and hardships with grace, resilience, and keeping our inner peace intact, adversity loses its power over us. When we fight what already *is*, we get into trouble.

The Universe is not seeking you out individually to make your life difficult. Just realizing that *everyone* has difficult situations arise throughout their lives, can allow you to more easily tap into your naturally resilient nature. All that is necessary to discover a solution that is right for you, in any moment of crisis, is to understand that it is already there, inside of you.

Without adversity, we could not appreciate all that we have, or learn how to view the chaotic world around us with clarity. By maintaining peaceful calm in the face of any storm, our inner self can remain intact, no matter what is going on around us. This can only be achieved with practice, just like any other skill.

When faced with a difficult challenge, stop for a moment to reflect, while listening carefully to what is going on inside of you. While the initial feeling you have, may be caused by thoughts of uncertainty, keep listening for an even deeper voice rising up within you. This voice can gently guide you toward peaceful calm and insight. It can also let you know with certainty that you will be alright, no matter what happens. The inner spirit is ageless and timeless. It cannot be destroyed by any circumstances, that may be found in the physical world.

Within you is a unique parcel of universal knowledge, which is always connected to the vast whole of the entire universe. You are far greater than your physical body and what is occurring around you in the earthly world. This understanding can give you all of the power and fortitude you need to see things, as they really are with the knowledge to act wisely in any given moment.

It is within moments of adversity that we find out who we really are; spiritual beings that have always been and will always be. We are here to experience all of the wonders of mortal life and master the challenge of being a spiritual being with the limitations of a physical body.

"We must let go of the life we have planned, so as to accept the one that is waiting for us."
-Joseph Campbell

Most of us plot and plan every single detail of what we want our life to be like. By doing this, we can miss out on the life that we already have; seeking to be somewhere other than where we are right now. By quieting your overly active mind in whatever method works for you, you can discover that it is within the context of stillness that your inner spirit can rise up to greet you, leading you gently into the authentic life that is waiting for you to embrace it.

"Never give up, for that is just the place and time that the tide will turn."
-Harriet Beecher Stowe

Just when things appear to be at their worst, the tide changes. Hold on as you move through the inevitable ups and downs that life brings your way. Dark days are your best teachers. Without them, you could not appreciate what it means to live in the light.

"Our life always expresses the result of our dominant thoughts."
-Soren Kirkegaard

The life you have created is based upon your dominant thoughts. When you fall out of toxic, habitual, *'what if'* thinking to begin focusing your attention on the present, your life becomes a reflection of those higher thoughts. If your thoughts are fixated on the past or are lost somewhere in the future, your life will be burdened with feelings of un-happiness, longing, frustration, and self-imposed stress. While we can-not control the hundreds of thousands of thoughts that we have each day, we can decide which ones deserve our attention and focus. Allow disturbing, negative thoughts to pass through you, without giving them a place to land and take root. Hold onto the positive thoughts and give them your focus and attention. Positive thoughts are the very foundation of happiness.

"Come out of the masses. Stand like a lion and live your life according to your own light."
-Osho

The courage to rise up and out of the masses of people, trying to force you to be who they want you to be, is the first step toward a meaningful life. Be the magnificent, unique person that you really are. As you rise up to take your place in the world, find the courage, within, to share your unique talents with the world. The world is waiting for you.

"No one can create negativity or stress within you. Only you can do that by virtue of how you process your world."
-Wayne Dyer

How we process the situations we encounter in life, makes all the difference in whether we see the glass as half full or half empty. No one has the power to impose negativity onto your life, unless you surrender your power over to them.

"If the ladder is not leaning against the right wall, every step we take just gets us to the wrong place faster."
-Stephen R. Covey

You may feel like you are going nowhere fast, as you search for answers to life's challenges, without any apparent direction. If you look within for answers, you will be able to know with certainty, exactly what you need to do.

"I am not what has happened to me. I am what I choose to become."
-Carl Jung

You are not what has happened to you. Any painful moment, in the past, is now only a memory. You are what you choose to be right now. Our destiny is not pre-determined by past moments. The only moment we ever really have is this moment right now. This moment is what defines you.

*"You have not lived today, until you have
done something for someone who can never repay you."*
-John Bunyan

Kindness is not only good for the recipient. Random acts of kindness profoundly affect the giver, placing them in contact with their authentic self. Our authentic self is the kind and loving being within us, that existed long before the day to day events of life contaminated our opinion of ourselves. Anonymous, random acts of kindness that cannot possibly be repaid, do more to uplift us than we can possibly imagine.

"There is a voice inside that doesn't use words. Listen."
-Rumi

It is when we are very quiet and not engaged in active thought, that who we really are rises up to enter into our consciousness. This voice does not use words to speak to us. To hear its promptings we must listen very intently. Allow time daily for your inner spirit to communicate with you. It is always there, willing and ready to greet you, even if you may doubt its existence.

"Learn how to see. Realize that everything connects to everything else."
-Leonardo da Vinci

Realizing that we are all connected to one another in this vast universe, allows us to look more kindly on one another, offer a helping hand, see more commonalities than differences, and to not be so easily offended. We are all connected, each of us an integral part of an eternal, greater whole.

"So, the single most vital step on your journey toward enlightenment is this; learn to dis-identify from your mind."
-Eckhart Tolle

If we can come to the realization that although we have a personal mind, we are *not* our mind, we will not take so seriously the millions of random thoughts that it constantly generates. When our personal mind rules us, we cannot find peace or any lasting happiness. Conversely, when our spirit is directing us, we remain connected to all of the wisdom of the universe. We are so much more than the limitations of our personal mind.

"There is force in the universe, which, if we permit it, will flow through us and produce miraculous results."
-Mahatma Gandhi

The force and sheer magnitude of the universe is incomprehensible to the human mind. Each being possesses its own unique piece of the universe within. Encoded in every cell is the wisdom of the universe attempting to gain the attention of the human mind, seeking to guide us our experience. If we allow our ageless and timeless spirit to be our guide, we can experience a truly magnificent metamorphosis.

"You forgive yourself by realizing that nobody can act beyond their level of consciousness.
-Eckhart Tolle

Forgiveness benefits the person offering forgiveness, far more than it does the perceived wrong doer. The act of forgiveness, no longer permits control over our emotions by another. Perhaps, the most challenging act of forgiveness is that of forgiving ourselves. Know deeply that no matter what we may have done, each of us was doing the best we could with the understanding we had, at the time. Once we increase our understanding, we can behave differently.

"Learning to distance yourself from all negativity is one of the greatest lessons to achieve inner peace."
-Roy Bennett

Negativity is like a cancer that spreads throughout every aspect of our lives. It is so incredibly easy to succumb to negativity. There is so much of it, as the world is passing through a darkened, chaotic phase of unbelievable depravity, and unbridled greed. Resist being pulled into its devastating grasp. Pay close attention to how you are feeling. Feelings are the barometer of your thoughts. Allow negative thoughts to pass through you without landing, while realizing that negativity is merely a thought that has no real power over us, unless we surrender ourselves over to it.

"And in this game of life, we all search for ourselves. When I say selves, I mean 'inner selves', the thing that created the life in the first place. Now, consciously, most of us are not aware of this. But if you're searching for happiness; if you're searching for tranquility; if you're searching just to have a nice, peaceful, loving, understanding life...in actual fact, you're searching for your inner-self." -Sydney Banks

28

Why Do We Experience Stress?

Perhaps, one of the most puzzling and plaguing issues of modern man is that of trying to understand what stress is, why we get it and what can be done about it. It has even infiltrated our modern vocabulary:

"I'm feeling so stressed out!"
"He is stressing me out!"
"This job is too stressful!"

You get the picture. When something is not providing us with a peaceful experience, we usually interpret the event as stress-inducing. In reality, what is actually happening is that, we are simply *perceiving* that events and circumstances have power over our emotions. As we begin to ruminate on negative thoughts, feelings automatically arise to support those thoughts. Feelings are, in reality, a very accurate gauge of our thoughts, at any given moment.

Our body will respond physiologically to stressful thoughts with a 'fight or flight' response. In turn, this response produces a cascade of physical effects; flushing, dilated pupils, increased heart rate, perspiring, increased blood pressure, cortisol and adrenaline release, that are accompanied by a strong urge to flee from the stressful situation. This physiologic response only serves to cement, even further, the flawed thinking that a particular event 'caused' us to experience these physical responses.

When these feelings of stress are believed to be coming from our job, our spouse, our children, or our families, this misunderstanding can become even more problematic. The need for a job with sufficient income to sustain us or to safeguard the love that we feel for our families, our spouse, and our children, can all dramatically complicate our feelings even further. It is, at this point, that many of us choose to wall off those troubling feelings, resulting in a collection of what can ultimately become a mountain of resentments.

This creates even more issues with the person or the event that we wrongly perceive, has actually *caused* these feelings. This scenario can become the vicious negative feedback loop that we commonly call 'stress'.

The reality is no person, event, circumstance, or place has any power to cause us stress.

This does not minimize, in any way, the fact that people, events, and circumstances can have significant impact on our lives. The actions of others can be misguided, cruel, and even, physically harmful. *What happens after any challenging event or situation is what is more impactful than the actual event.* During any threatening event or circumstance, our amazing innate instincts kick in, resulting in instinctive self-preservation. In other words, if our life is being imminently threatened, we will take immediate protective action instinctively. While we may be over-powered by an assailant and physically harmed, no matter how horribly we are treated in that moment, the event, itself, does not last forever. At some point, it is over and becomes a memory.

Maintaining perspective about what happens next is the most

important part of any traumatic experience. Once you are physically safe, processing the event can overwhelm you, even paralyzing your thoughts, if you permit it. It is important to understand that no matter how awful an event may have been at the time that it was occurring, it was never something that you deserved, or could control. No one ever deserves to be harmed. Equally important to understand is that, the person who harmed you then, has no power over you right now. The event is now in the past, only residing in your memory. Mistakenly believing that actions in the past have any power to control your life now, is how long-term, chronic stress can begin.

Wishing that traumatic events in your life had never occurred, or believing that if you just had a better job, a different partner, more obedient children, had a million dollars, or that if you lived in a different location, then horrible things would not happen to you, are all very destructive, self-defeating patterns of thinking. This mindset does not improve your life in any way and cannot alter the past. While there may be transient moments in your life when things may seem better after you obtain the latest object of your desire, happy feelings from external circumstances simply cannot last.

It is the mistaken belief that one's happiness and well-being is dependent on outside events, that causes all of our unhappiness in life.

In reality, our life is an inside-out experience. It may seem that events, outside of us, are causing our thoughts and feelings, but they are not. Events never have that power. Your perception of life comes from within you, never from outside of you. When you understand that life is really an inside-out process, events and circumstances begin to lose their 'power' over you. It becomes much easier to see things as they really are, when you understand the true nature of how life works. It is vital to defend and protect your inner-self from the misguided belief that external circumstances have any real power to have an effect on who you are, spiritually. They do not.

While everyone is subject to difficulty from time to time,

circumstances simply cannot dictate who you are internally. We come into this life hard-wired with the resilience we need, to weather life's storms that come and go. If you pause for just a moment, to make contact with your inner spirit when challenges arise, you will be able to know, with certainty, what you need to do next. Understanding this is very empowering. You already possess all the power you need to overcome any challenge. It is by surrendering to imaginary control by external circumstances, that creates our suffering and stress.

How do we manage stressful thoughts?

While thoughts are random associations based on memory and conditioning that we cannot control, they do not have power in and of themselves to take over our lives. Our resilient spirit possesses the necessary power to bridle any focus that we may be tempted to give to destructive thoughts. When unhealthy thoughts are ignored, they are extinguished, allowing new thoughts to arise that can break this self-destructive pattern. Merely realizing that a destructive thought pattern is just a thought, is often enough to interrupt the downward spiral.

When we are stuck in the *"Our lives would be better if..."* way of thinking, pay very close attention to those thoughts and feelings. Know deeply that this way of thinking is never the truth. Life is only ever experienced in this moment that we are in right now. It is not found in the past or the future. Spending our lives, dwelling on the past, with no hope of changing events that have already occurred, or alternately ruminating on uncertain future scenarios that may never come to pass, rob us of being in the only place where life occurs: the here and now.

Life is truly a glorious adventure, meant to be directed by the spirit that resides within our mortal frame. Worlds without end are within us, waiting to unfold. All we need to do to understand this universal wisdom, is to listen intently to the spirit within, that is patiently waiting for us to acknowledge it, and permit it to guide us.

Index of Paintings by Steven D. Lyons

IN ORDER OF APPEARANCE

- *Songs from another Universe 2409x1594*, Acrylic on Canvas (book cover)
- *Super Moon*, 30 x 30, Acrylic on Canvas
- *Red Dory At Rest*, 24 x 48, Acrylic on Canvas
- *Portrait of Three boys, Refugees in Flight*, 36 x 24, Acrylic on Canvas
- *Looking Up*, Acrylic on Canvas
- *Crash #3*, 36 x 60, Acrylic on Canvas
- *Waiting for Daylight*, Acrylic on Canvas
- *Painted Ladies Three Portraits*, 36 x 36, Acrylic on Canvas
- *Painted Ladies Take a Garden Tour*, Acrylic on Canvas
- *Spring Breaker*, 36 x 36, Acrylic on Canvas
- *October Sonnet 2*, 36 x 36, Acrylic on Canvas
- *Sister; I had my creator give me blue eyes, so that you might accept me*, 40 x 30, Acrylic and Gold Leaf on Canvas
- *Solitude*, Acrylic on Canvas
- *As Morning Awakens*, 36 x 48, Acrylic and Gold Leaf on Canvas
- *Moon River*, 30 x 40, Acrylic on Canvas
- *Sunset Sail #2*, 24 x 36, Acrylic and Copper Leaf on Canvas
- *Sails at Evening*, 18 x 36, Acrylic on Canvas
- *Joe De Vivre*, 48 x 36, Acrylic on Canvas
- *Fleeing Damascus*, Acrylic on Canvas
- *Golden Forest*, 24 x 48, Acrylic and Gold and Copper Leaf on Canvas
- *Under Your Spell*, 40 x 40, Acrylic on Canvas

- *Opus in Blue #2*, 30 x 48, Acrylic on Canvas
- *Women At the Stream*, 24 x 36, Acrylic on Canvas
- *Romancing the Dunes*, 30 x 40, Acrylic on Canvas
- *Man in Le Corbusier*, 24 x 36, Print
- *Tranquility in Blue*, 36 x 48, Acrylic on Canvas
- *The Morning Alights*, 24 x 36, Acrylic on Canvas
- *The Memories of Me*, 36 x 36, Acrylic on Canvas
- *Figurines on the Staircase*, 48 x 36, Acrylic on Canvas
- *Still Life with Oranges*, 48 x 24, Acrylic on Canvas
- *Morning Romance*, 48 x 60, Acrylic on Canvas
- *Dancer in Repose*, 40 x 30, Acrylic on Canvas
- *A Day In Late Autumn*, Acrylic on Canvas
- *The Automation of Man*, 48 x 24, Acrylic on Canvas
- *Full Moon Over the Water*, Acrylic on Canvas
- *She Stayed Happy By Remembering the Moon and the Stars*, 30 x 40, Acrylic on Canvas
- *Birch Trees In Moonlight 2*, Acrylic on Canvas
- *The Dreamer*, 40 x 30, Acrylic, Gold and Copper Leaf
- *The Girls in the Band*, 48 x 30, Acrylic on Canvas
- *Dancing Clouds Over the Beach*, 30 x 30, Acrylic on canvas
- *Red Dune in Grayscale*, 15 x 30, Acrylic on Canvas
- *The Silver Tree*, 20 x 20, Acrylic and Graphite with Gold, Copper and Silver Leaf on Canvas
- *The Two Faces of Mary*, 36 x 24, Acrylic on Canvas
- *Path to a View #9*, 24 x 48, Acrylic on Canvas
- *Morning Flats*, Acrylic on Canvas
- *Women and the Universe*, 48 x 72, Acrylic on Canvas
- *Conversations*, 36 x 24, Acrylic on Canvas
- *Can I Join You*, 24 x 24, Acrylic on Canvas
- *Society's Women*, 36 x 24, Acrylic on Canvas
- *Marsh in Black and White*, 40 x 40, Acrylic on Canvas
- *The Old Priest*, 30 x 24, Acrylic on Canvas
- *Breathe*, 30 x 48, Acrylic on Canvas
- *Entering the Forest*, 20 x 16, Acrylic on Canvas

- *The Walk Home,* 24 x 36, Acrylic on Canvas
- *The Oasis,* Acrylic on Canvas
- *Snow in Pines,* 24 x 24, Acrylic on Canvas
- *The Portal,* 40 x 60, Acrylic on Canvas
- *Winter,* 24x 48
- *The Village #2,* 30 x 40, Acrylic on Canvas

About the Artist

The late, Steve Lyons, was an artist and gallery owner, based out of Chatham, Massachusetts. His work became some of the most recognized art in the USA and Europe. He was highly regarded for creating what is internationally known as 'sculptural paintings'. This breakthrough technique utilized heavy *impasto* to create heightened dimensionality on the canvas, and captured the attention of critics, collectors, artists, and the general public across the globe.

In 2016, Lyons was named one of the Top 5 Expressionist Artists in the World, by the American Art Awards. Steve Lyons was the first American to win the shared exhibition prize at the Stadtgalerie, in Westerland, Germany. In 2014, he was the first American awarded private mentorship with Finland's premier living artist and designer, Markku Piri.

He has exhibited his paintings all over the world, including Freising (Munich), Berlin, La Paz (Mexico), Poznan (Poland), and Paris, among other locations across Europe. His work has also been exhibited in New Haven and Old Greenwich, Connecticut, Boston, Massachusetts, and Cincinnati, Ohio, and is held in collections by a number of individuals and institutions. Lyons was born and raised in Portsmouth, Ohio, located on the northern banks of the Ohio River.

He began painting as a child and by age eight, had won his first competition in Canton, Ohio. He earned a B.A. at Eastern Kentucky University, and an M.A. at Louisiana State University—where he majored in journalism, minored in art, and was a Walter Hitesman Scholarship recipient. Lyons lived in New York City for eight years before calling New England home. His primary residency prior to his death, was in Chatham, MA, although he traveled extensively to Europe. Steve Lyon's remaining art collection is privately held by his family, after his untimely death in March, 2021.

Elizabeth M. Lykins, PA-C, MPAS is a medical provider, transformational coach, and digital products publisher, currently residing in the Bay area of California. With extensive training and experience in emergency medicine, in addition to her coaching services, she provides medical care for patients in an urgent care setting.

Her transformational coaching services are primarily based upon the Three Principles approach by Sydney Banks, but she is also influenced by Eckhart Tolle, Don Miguel Ruiz, and other mindfulness-based spiritual teachers. She has formal training in the Three Principles approach by renowned coach and author, Jamie Smart.

Elizabeth has received training and multiple certifications in neurolinguistic programming (NLP), EFT (Emotional Freedom Techniques), hypnotherapy, CBT-I (Cognitive Behavioral Therapy – Insomnia), TIME techniques, and Success and Life Coaching.

She holds a master's degree in Physician Assistant Studies in Emergency Medicine from the University of Nebraska Medical Center, a bachelor's degree in Clinical Health Sciences, and certification in medicine, from the University of Washington School of Medicine. She additionally holds an Associate of Arts degree from Shawnee State University, where she trained in respiratory therapy and practiced as a Registered Respiratory Therapist (RRT), before attending medical school.

Elizabeth is the author of *Letter to Caroline*, under the *nom de plume* of Elizabeth Fannin (copyright © 2009). She is the publisher, editor, and founder of mindfulness-based digital magazine, *Magnificent Metamorphosis Magazine – Inspiration for Positive Change*. She contributes articles regularly to *Tips on Inside-Out Living Newsletter* (LinkedIn).

She enjoys travel, music, dance, martial arts, volunteering in local animal shelters, the many amenities of the Bay Area, and spending time with her daughter and their cats.